On the Wings of a North Wind

On the Wings
of a North Wind

The Waterfowl and Wetlands
of America's Inland Flyways

Michael Furtman

Stackpole Books

Published by
STACKPOLE BOOKS
Cameron and Kelker Streets
P.O. Box 1831
Harrisburg, PA 17105

Printed in the United States of America

First Edition

10 9 8 7 6 5 4 3 2 1

Photo section designed by Marcia Lee Dobbs

Library of Congress Cataloging-in-Publication Data

Furtman, Michael.
   On the wings of a north wind : the waterfowl and wetlands of
America's inland flyways / Mike Furtman. — 1st ed.
      p.   cm.
   ISBN 0-8117-1787-9
   1. Ducks—United States—Migration. 2. Geese—United States—
Migration. 3. Ducks—Canada—Migration. 4. Geese—Canada—
Migration. 5. Waterfowl management—United States. 6. Waterfowl
management—Canada. 7. Wetlands—United States. 8. Wetlands—
Canada. I. Title. II. Title: America's inland flyways.
QL696.A52F87   1991
598.4'1—dc20   91-8062
                                                          CIP

For Mary Jo,
whose enduring love and endless patience I often test

Contents

Foreword

This book is about one man's dream to travel with waterfowl down the once and future flyways of interior North America. "This trip wasn't intended to be a quest for America," Mike Furtman writes. "Steinbeck and Moon have done that already. This is a quest for waterfowl, and maybe a bit more."

Maybe quite a bit more, as it turns out, for *On the Wings of a North Wind* is also about the people Furtman meets along the way (including a band of hostile Indians!) and the need for all of us, whether we know it or not, to be part of nature.

The book's strength stems from Furtman's abilities as a writer and his innocence: "I am thirty-five," this Minnesotan says, "and a homebody. I have never been south of Des Moines or north of nearby southern Ontario. I have never been away from home, alone, for more than a week or two. Now here I am, tooling along the highway, heading for who-knows-where."

Without, perhaps, realizing it, Furtman taps into the power of *mythology*, as the late religious scholar and anthropologist Joseph Campbell meant that word. The story of an innocent seeking experience with only an empathetic beast to share his journey is as old as the oldest native American legend and as new as the *Star Wars* trilogy.

Questing is uniquely masculine. Most women prefer returning to places where they've been secure and happy. Men, on the other hand, are forever drawn to frontiers, to the unknown.

Wildfowling is a young man's game, and "romantic aesthetes" (to use writer-wildfowler Vance Bourjaily's description of duck hunters) revel in prevailing over the adverse weather, even danger, of our best mornings in the marsh. Few women share our passion for this most rigorous—and if you're careless, most ruthless—form of bird hunting.

Joseph Campbell once remarked that the male students in his classes at Sarah Lawrence College were always asking themselves the same two questions: "How does it work?" and "What does it mean?" By contrast, he said, his female students were always asking, "What will this do for me?" This is because women (even the word *woman* refers to the female sex's procreative potential) are the custodians of our species' continuity, and few see much advantage in the cold, wet realm in which ducks, dogs, and certain males seem to thrive—unless by sharing a blind, a girl may make her father proud, or a young woman may find herself a duck-hunting husband like Dad.

Ever since our species evolved a capacity for contemplating the meaning of life in the face of inevitable death, boys have intuitively sought passage into manhood through enduring some ritual of hardship or suffering. For countless generations, this meant war. War, says William Broyles, Jr., creator of the television series *China Beach*, "is, for men, at some terrible level the closest thing to what childbirth is for women; the initiation into the power of life and death."

War, however, no longer provides legitimate rites of passage, because survival in war no longer depends on skill and courage. Modern wars are more liable to kill noncombatants than soldiers, and death is by remote control or accident.

Men, however, have been hunters longer than we've been warriors, and by both custom and self-imposed regulation, the best wildfowlers today hunt with a minimum of technology, knowing that the fewer gadgets we pack, the more likely we'll find the epiphany we seek. Our canine companions link us to nature and our misty origins in the Pleistocene marshes.

Like Mike and his Lab, Rascal, we travel lean, and we learn. And like the two Arkansas boys they meet, we often do "lookin' mo' den huntin'," but the *lookin'* in this book is worth a lot.

George Reiger
Locustville, Virginia

Acknowledgments

There are so many people who aided me in this adventure that I am loath to attempt to thank them all for fear of forgetting someone. But I will try.

My thanks go first to Sally Atwater of Stackpole Books for the chance to do this trip and book. Thanks also to Jennifer Byrne for her skillful editing.

Along the way many biologists and other interested professionals shared with me their knowledge and love of waterfowl, as well as their concerns. Some of them are Ross Melinchuk, Ron Stromstad, Leo Kirsch, Len McDaniel, Dick Gersib, Frank Bellrose, Scott Yaich, and Dave Hall. To each of you: I hope I portrayed both your work and your hopes accurately. Thanks also to the many others who took the time to talk to me and whose knowledge, if not names or words, appears in this book.

Traveling alone can be arduous. I gratefully acknowledge the assistance of Ralph Henn of the Canadian Consulate Office, Gerard Makuch of Saskatchewan Tourism, Dennis Maksymetz of Manitoba Tourism, and Mary Emanuel of Nebraska Tourism. They made my travels easier and more pleasant.

The Federal Cartridge Company supplied me with their fine ammunition. Dr. and Mrs. William Rudie generously granted me the use of their wonderful Wisconsin cabin. Thank you.

I must also acknowledge those who spent some time with me in the field, whether toting shotguns after upland birds in grassy swards, sharing the sunrise with me in a goose pit or duck blind, or engaging a lonesome traveler in conversation at a duck camp. Jack Cox, Tom Rosdail, Bob Jaskinksi, Jon Gollmar, Bill Pearce, Morris Nielsen, and Dale Brock all made the trip more enjoyable and memorable. Thanks.

Thanks also to Rascal—a fine companion. I wish a belated Nobel Prize on the creator of the Labrador retriever.

Finally, to three very special examples of what is good about the human race, Ray Heupel, Rick Hampton, and Jesse Duet; thank you for your kindness to Rascal and me and for all your efforts on behalf of the ducks.

Prologue

The wind came like a wolf from the north, the breath of winter in its maw. Frost painted the cattails with a glistening veneer. In the morning, when the sun climbed over the golden prairie horizon, the feather-crystaled skim ice tinkled as it melted.

A great uneasiness stirred on the prairie marsh. Ducks took wing, first in twos and threes, then tens, then twenties, testing newly feathered wings in the joy of flight, flashing a sunlit semaphore of the coming of winter. The ducks had been gathering since the first males had grouped for the molt, the awkward, flightless three weeks when they shed and grew anew their plumes. Some of the restless ducks were feeling the lift of wind on their wings for the first time; this their first autumn of life. They had gathered in large flocks for protection by virtue of number. One hundred pairs of eyes sense danger well, two hundred even better yet.

There were females, too, on this cold October day. Somber hens in tawny camouflage had marched their broods through drought and danger to this marsh. The chicks had grown to nearly full size, and the hens had little more to do with them. All the ducks now fed heavily, anticipating the coming migration by building reserves of fat for the grueling flight.

When the days began growing shorter and the north wind blew clear and crisp, the mixed flocks separated into groups of their own kind. An urgency of light and weather and hormones stirred the slough.

One of the hens in this pothole was a wary mallard, a wise old bird who had made many flights to the wintering grounds where she swam and fed amid the buttressed cypress trees. She had arrived in spring with her gaudy greenhead mate, the one she had picked from many suitors, the one whose nuptial displays told her he was as wise and wary as she and would make a fine partner. They flew to the place where she had been born and where generations of her female relatives had nested and raised their young.

Her pothole was similar to the millions of other potholes that once had graced the prairie. Shallow and fertile, it was free of ice early in spring, full of nourishment, and near broad grassy plains thick with places a clever hen could hide her precious nest.

There was a difference this year. All along their flight north, pursuing the receding winter, they had had difficulty locating water. A decade of drought, now at its worst, had dried the prairie-pothole region. The hen led her mate north, using landscape to guide them when there was light, stars when darkness overcame them. She flew unerringly as the mosaic world whirled beneath them: roiling prairie streams brown with the melt of spring, black fallow farm fields, and frighteningly brilliant nighttime cities. The pair moved in spurts on favorable south winds, from wetland to lake to stream to pond, consistently heading north. Her homing instinct was strong, and the memory of her race ran deep.

Moved by the need to reproduce, the mated pair winged on, looking for the next ice-free slough. When at last she arrived at the spot that was her natal wetland and that of her mother and her grandmother, she cupped her wings and led her gaudy partner out of the weary April sky, low, low, across the winter beaten cattails and bullrushes, slowly, gladly, to the waiting water below.

One hundred years ago her ancestors had found here an abundance of nesting sites. Bison had dotted the range, the bellowing brown cows heavy with calves that would soon be ruddy, romping miniatures, and tall grass had bowed in waves of weathered gray as all life awaited the lushness of spring.

Even in her ten years of returning to this pothole, the hen had seen many changes. Each year there had been less water, partly because of the drought and partly because the snows that did come were blown from the bare earthen fields that now surrounded the marsh, the fields left fallow all winter, tortured by the winds.

Each year, too, the farmer that called the land his had crept his plow ever nearer to the wetland's margin. When he had first broken the sod he had been satisfied to leave the rolling hills around the pothole in grass, but more recently he had decided to risk erosion and to each year plow the steep grades ever nearer the water.

Feeding in the spring-warmed waters, building strength and reserves from the bodies of the writhing invertebrates, the hen and drake prepared for nesting. Each evening the hen would lead her mate on low flights over the neighboring landscape in a search of a nest site.

Finally, she settled for a low spot in the grassy margin surrounding the pothole. She lined the shallow bowl she scraped in the moist earth with bits of plants and down from her breast, and one day at a time, one egg a day, she laid her clutch.

One morning, when she waddled down to the marsh to drink and feed, she noticed that her mate was gone. He had departed for a distant marsh to join other drakes. Alone in mid-April, she braved weather and detection atop the eight buff-green eggs.

She had been on her eggs for almost two weeks, the days lengthening, the weather warming. Sneaking through the dusk a fox spied her pothole and came down the narrow margin of grass, its nose working the wind, hunger in a red fur coat. Nervously, the hen watched its stealthy approach and only reluctantly made her escape when the red blur made a lunge for her. Quacking in fear and anxiety, she flew off to the pothole while the fox consumed her eggs.

With no mate, yet with nature's strong desire welling, she protested loudly on the pothole, hoping to find another drake. A young mallard, unmated in this his first adult spring, came to her, and although she was not enthusiastic about the choice, she allowed the coupling to take place. When she laid her second clutch of eggs, a hundred yards down the wetland margin from the first site, she mustered only six.

Her first nest had been laid in early April, for in her was the instinct that early breeders had the best success. The second effort came in May, and as the heat of summer began to blanket the prairie, she sat on her eggs near the dwindling pothole. No fox came this time.

As sweltering July neared, the hen was caring for a peeping brood. Within hours of the drying of the yellow-downed chicks, she had marched them single file to the pothole, a milestone journey for the tiny, tumbling legs. For days they fed, until it was apparent that the water would soon be completely gone, swallowed by the gaping cracks that were appearing on the salty mud or fading into the sky as it evaporated. No rain had fallen since the hen had arrived.

A three-mile march across the wheat fields, over gravel roads, and perilously near hunting predators took the hen and her waddling brood to the very same large pothole where both her mates had gone to loaf and molt. When she and her brood slid relieved into the water, they joined the safety of the group and found the lushness of the fertile pothole that would sustain them through the last days of summer. They were the lucky ones. Across all the prairie many more nests had failed then had succeeded. When autumn came, the ducks would be lucky to have replaced themselves, one for one.

August came and went in long, sunny days of preening on mudflats and pleasant, golden hours of dabbling and feeding. The bond between the hen and chicks lessened as the birds grew. By the end of the month, they were nearly full-grown and ready for flight.

September brought hints of the demise of summer. Flocks of pintails and blue-winged teal left before the end of the month, despite the availability of food and the lingering temperate days. Flocks of local mallards, as well as gadwalls and wigeon, moved onto this bigger marsh until, as each night fell and another morning dawned, the surface of the water was dotted with more and more birds. Raucous cries, the bantering of ducks, were heard at daybreak.

Wave after wave of *peent*ing sandpipers arrived, twisting in flight or strutting on the mudflats. Blackbirds swarmed the cattails, then rose like dark thoughts to feed in the wheat fields. Groups of geese, mostly local birds, began to appear, then sat and scanned the sky for the big flocks from the north. Nervously, the ducks watched the shadows of prairie hawks and falcons as these birds, too, began to move in numbers.

Clusters of ducks at dusk and dawn, black whistling wedges against the sky, large flocks looking like living columns of smoke, spiraled earthward to scavenge the heads of grain missed during the autumn harvest. The days shortened, and an urge as strong as the one that had brought the ducks north was triggered deep within them.

When the first winds howled from the arctic wastes and the nights spoke with the creaking of new ice, a change came over the birds. Daily the fleeing arrivals came from the marshlands far distant, the bite of winter at their tails. Daily eager groups departed, though the number on this lake continued to rise, ever bolstered by emigrants.

The phragmites, yellow cane in the sun, fine flags whipping in the wind, bowed toward the south. Cattails rattled in the same north wind.

October came. Slate gray clouds hid the azure sky. Short days added to the quickening pace. An uneasiness stirred, not one of fear or dread, but one of anticipation. The cold meant winter, a lack of food, frozen ponds, death. But it also meant flight south to warm days, a flight to something good. A change was coming over the earth and the ducks.

The migration south was nearing.

I am wheeling across Minnesota. It is the third week in September, and I am passing through the familiar forests of home, aspen and birch beginning to show the change of the season in a bath of yellow, a happy contrast against the pine and spruce. The sky is blue and it is a perfect day, the morning highway devoid of traffic, the air crisp, my Labrador retriever by my side trying her best to knock over the cup of scalding coffee I hold in my right hand.

The truck cruises smoothly, the weight of the camper and all my supplies helping to smooth the bumps from the road. I am self-contained, comfortable in that I can go anywhere and need nothing, comfortable in the companionship of Rascal, her big, black head resting on my elbow, amber eyes searching me.

Across the state I wind, down Highway 210, an admirable highway banked by forest, a sinuous path through the world. I have a Strauss waltz on the tape deck, and as I float on the music I see a hawk soaring above a farm field, as if he, too, were a part of the musical strain.

And yet this perfect day cannot hide my apprehension. The warm dog cannot stem it. My enthusiasm for this trip cannot temper it. Let's face it. I'm a little worried.

Let me tell you what I'm up to. I am leaving my home to seek waterfowl. I am in love with waterfowl. I have spent my life trundling into swamps and paddling down rivers and across lakes, burdened by decoys, guns, cameras, and hip boots, parting the dark night with flashlight beams in the hopes of being where waterfowl might come. I'll walk in boot-sucking bogs and endure rain, snow, and cold to see them come spraddle-legged into the decoys, watch them fly by without giving me even a glance, hear them split the air in a gasp as they come from nowhere, glimpse their flash of wings in the sunlight, and listen to them quack in the fog. And all of this would have been enough, forever, until recently.

The world has been changing. Not in the way it has for eons. Not in the slow manner of evolution, with small changes over long periods of time. Not with nature taking the lead. The world has changed for the worse. I do not know all the reasons why, but I do know that the ducks do not come as they once did—there are fewer of them and the species I see are less diverse. I have heard of destruction of habitat, of drought, of pesticides, of predators and poaching—of any number of reasons that ducks are in trouble. But I must know for myself, to see all this firsthand. So I have set off, to drive from Saskatchewan to Louisiana, to try to understand

North by West

not only these problems but also something of the birds themselves. To be a part of the migration.

All my adult life I have dreamed of traveling with the ducks and geese, feeling the same rush of the north wind at my back, knowing that it portends of winter. I wanted their sense to be mine, to feel their urge to go wherever they go. I needed to experience this marvelous migration firsthand and cold, tired, or hungry. Only then, I felt, could I understand what it meant to ride on the wings of a north wind.

Now here I am, living that dream. A quest? Maybe. I want answers. I want—need—to know that the ducks are all right, that there is hope for the future, that this important heritage, this thread in the fabric of my life, is intact.

So I am apprehensive. North America's waterfowl population, specifically ducks, has never been so low. Never. The year 1989 was the driest on record. When the prairies dried up, the ducks could not reproduce. Farmers in duck country used this as an opportunity to burn the dry potholes, plowing them up so that when the water did return, the ducks could not. It was maddening—and not just a little scary.

I'm afraid for other reasons, too. I am thirty-five and a homebody. I have never been south of Des Moines or north of nearby southern Ontario. I have never been away from home, alone, for more than a week or two. Now here I am, tooling along the highway, heading for who-knows-where.

The whole of North America lies before me. It will be a grand autumn, I tell myself, with mornings in the marsh, decoys before me, and a wet Labrador at my side.

To the north of the highway flows the Mississippi, and we follow it west and south until, at Brainerd, we cross this mighty river. It, too, is making a migration; the water flowing by me will reach the Louisiana bayous before I do. But I will see it there, and I will cross the river again and again before my trip is done.

Tonight I will camp somewhere on the North Dakota prairie. Finding a pothole would be nice. I could park the camper next to it and, I hope, listen to the happy sound of ducks chuckling in the dark. But will I find such a place?

The prairie began in western Minnesota. Clear streams and dark forest gave way to slow rivers and woodlots. Farms grew in size, and the rolling and rocky landscape gradually became sandy and smooth. Finally, the rich soil of the true prairie lay before me.

With each mile, I wheeled deeper into the American West, that great magnet that had drawn many with its promise of freedom and expansiveness. At Moorhead, Minnesota, I crossed the Red River as it flowed slowly to the north on its long journey to Hudson's Bay. Fargo, North Dakota, lay sprawling along the interstate, a conglomeration of truck stops, strip eateries, and dust. In the heat of the late afternoon, I felt as if I had just entered hell. I pushed the pick-up through the city, wanting to see an end to people and to feel the openness of the prairie.

Eastern North Dakota is flat but not featureless. The country rolls, like a sea, until at times I felt as if I were surfing across a great, wheat-bound ocean.

Rascal began to pant. I rolled the window down and opened the vents, aiming the louvres at the dog. Her wet black nose found them, and she inched toward the breeze. She looked at me anxiously. I knew what she wanted.

Stunted trees and concrete buildings greeted us at the rest stop. Dust swirled in the afternoon heat as we shuffled through the sun-seared grass, stiff as wire and just as lovely.

A highway department crew was working in the nearby ditch. Rascal, seeing potential playmates, ran over before I could stop her. I called, kicked into high gear, and caught up with her just as she startled a workman laying pipe.

"Jesus!" he proclaimed, looking up at me. Well, I do have a beard.

"Scared the hell out of me," he went on. Rascal was doing the butt-first dog dance along his leg, hoping to get scratched. He granted her wish, while I studied the open earth.

"Been dry, awful dry," said the laborer, poking the wall of the ditch with the tip of his shovel. The soil flowed like sand.

The earth's cross section told a clear story. At the top was wiry, sun-seared grass, its fibrous roots woven into a mat. Beneath it for perhaps two inches the earth was brown, holding some moisture. But below that lay the story of the decade in the prairie. Drought. Brown soil gave way to gray, dry dust.

"Been hard on the crops?"

"Terrible. Worst in years. My daddy's a farmer and he and my brother are just scraping along. Don't know what'll happen if this drought doesn't break soon. Took this job 'cause there ain't no money in farmin'. Not when you're just raisin' dust."

A backhoe labored down the ditch toward us. "Better move your dog. Where you headed?"

Rascal and I scrambled up the ditch to the grassy top. "Headed west tonight. Going to look for a place to camp near Chase Lake. Know the place?"

"Nope. Good luck. Nice dog you have there. Does she hunt?"

"You bet," I said, waving.

I watered the dog, she drinking in long, satisfying slurps, water running out the back corners of her jowls. She looked up, happy. When she was through I took the remainder of slobbered water over to the grass and poured it on the soil. No sense in wasting it on the blacktop. It disappeared almost instantly.

I grabbed a soda from the cooler, loaded the dog into the truck, buckled up, and hit the expressway. Like the prairie and the dog, I too was parched. Dust clung to every surface of the truck. You could have planted crops on my eyeglasses. I broke open the soda, felt it burn my throat clear, wiped my dusty glasses on my shirt, and headed west.

I woke up suddenly. In the blackness of the camper I could sense the black dog standing over me. *Harummp. Harummppp. Harrummmppp.*

I grabbed Rascal. Her entire body was heaving, her face only inches from mine. She was going to throw up.

Finding her collar, I tried to aim her toward the openness next to the bunk. But fighting my pull on the collar was too much. She heaved. It flapped wet against the sleeping bag, up my chest, and into my face. She heaved again. It hit me once more, splattered off my chest, and drenched the camper wall, bunk, sleeping bag, and pillow. I tossed her from the bunk and she cowered in the darkness near the door.

"You stupid mutt!" I screamed, leaping from the bunk. I slipped in puke. Flinging open the camper door, I launched the dog into the early-dawn darkness.

One hell of a way to wake up. I surveyed the damage, got out some paper toweling, and began to mop up. Vomit was everywhere. At least the green-brown mixture of dog food and grass wasn't smelly. It could have been worse. She *could* have eaten some dead critter before upchucking.

A half hour later, bunk and sleeping gear scrubbed, I got dressed and went outside to look for Rascal. She was sitting not far from the camper. Although she didn't run away, she was not sure that she wanted me to approach her.

"Come here, girl."

She came, tail low but wagging, as forlorn-looking as any creature could look. I knelt down. She rubbed against me.

"It's okay, girl. You couldn't help it." The dog was very happy to find out she was going to live.

No doubt she had eaten the wiry prairie grass the night before. I had let her run loose while I had visitors. In my underwear and climbing into the bunk, tired and ready for sleep, I had suddenly become aware of bright lights in the dark. A voice boomed out at the door. "Game wardens! We'd like to talk to you!"

Scrambling into some clothes, I opened the door while the dog threatened with low growls.

"Told you he was from Minnesota," the older of the two uniformed men said, flashlight on my license plate.

"Howdja know that?" asked the other, stealing words from me.

"Why, he's camped beneath the only damn tree in sight! They always do."

We laughed. I asked them in and explained what I was doing there. They were serving as security for the dedication the next day and were camped nearby when they spotted my lights. We talked and drank a half bottle of scotch. And that was probably when Rascal, running black and free in the Dakota night, ate something that ended up seeing the light of day again.

Now that we were up, Rascal and I walked to the top of a grassy knoll near where we had camped. In the east a cold sun was rising quickly, bathing the prairie and then Chase Lake in cold yellow light. I guessed that the temperature was twenty, maybe twenty-five degrees. The grasses were laced with frost and the pothole near camp was rimmed in ice. Phragmites glistened with white diamonds.

Away on the lake we heard geese warming up. Nearby, a *whoosh* of wings alerted us to passing ducks. They circled the pothole, and we stood at attention. Mallards. On the water a hidden hen quacked. A Susie on the wing asked instructions like a pilot to an air traffic controller. Finding the breeze under their wings, the eight or ten mallards locked up, swung into the pothole, and disappeared from our sight behind cattails just as their landing gear dropped. There was the hiss of water on splayed webbing.

Turning to the sunrise again, I looked across the expanse of Chase Lake. A dirt road separated us from the lake—as did a barbed-wire fence. A sign proclaimed the National Wildlife Refuge of which Chase Lake is a part, and I watched and listened as the waterfowl and sandhill cranes began their dawn greetings.

Ducks are early risers. They get up and about first, fanning out in search of food. Their passing is almost silent unless one is lucky enough to be near their destination.

Sandhill cranes are something else. When they arise, shortly after the ducks, they launch themselves in waves, the big ungainly-looking birds passing by in vee formation. Not only are they hard to miss on the wing, but they let the world know they are coming. In an almost electronic-sounding *herrrt* (screw your voice up like a teenage boy's cracking, and roll your Rs), sandhills proclaim their comings and goings. Even if they flew mute, their seven-foot wingspan would give them away.

Geese keep bankers' hours. Rarely are they up and about until after the ducks and cranes are long gone. When they do arise, however, they enthusiastically greet the morning with a grand cacophony of honking and barking.

In this frosty morning, Rascal stood absolutely rigid with excitement, straining to hear the birds, her brown eyes scanning the horizon. Silent small flocks of mallards, pintails, and gadwalls worked the purple sky. The cranes were up and talking. The geese remained in slumber.

Sorry I had been so hard on my dog, I reached down and scratched her ears. Cold air slithered under my collar. A shiver ran down my spine. A cup of coffee would taste very good, I thought.

We returned to the camper. Opening the door, I motioned Rascal in. She looked at me hesitantly. I could guess what she was thinking.

"Come on, girl. Kennel up."

She did, I did, and we had breakfast.

About seven o'clock I heard a commotion on the hillside. Trucks were rumbling up the grassy knoll to the north of our camp, circling, in wagon train fashion, an enormous circus-type tent. Today was to be a festive occasion.

Here in the midst of the North Dakota prairie was to be an experiment of sorts. For the first time in living memory agricultural interests and wildlife management in the United States were to strike a deal. Since the first immigrant sliced the prairie turf, there has been an adversarial relationship between the homesteaders and the native plants and creatures. When this nation's population was much smaller and the farms less mechanized, mankind and nature were more or less in balance. Creatures seen as threats or as competitors, such as the bison, prairie elk, prairie wolf, and plains grizzly, were eliminated. The pronghorn antelope survived in reduced numbers, and the deer fared well on woodlots and cultivated crops.

So, too, did the waterfowl remain in numbers for a while, their wetland habitats too difficult for nonmechanized farming to invade. Then, with the development of powerful machinery to plow and drain vast acreage and government money and assistance in designing the drainage, the hard-working farmers applied their diligence to ridding the prairie of pesky wildlife once and for all.

Now man and beast had come to an impasse on the drought-burned prairie. The water that had been life to ducks and other wild creatures, as well as to the farmers and their crops, had simply quit coming. Crop yields dropped. So did wildlife broods. Staggered by the decade of record heat and minimal precipitation, both man and animal teetered on the brink of complete failure.

Perhaps it was this crisis, with a bit of empathy thrown in, that had led to this day's event. Maybe some common sense played a role. In any case, landowners, ranchers, and farmers were being plied with incentives by wildlife managers to make room for wildlife, particularly for prairie-nesting, water-needing birds. This event, staged as a feel-good kickoff for participants and a show for the mass media, was to herald a new era in land stewardship.

With the full light of day now bathing the prairie, I tied Rascal up near the camper and walked the quarter mile to the hilltop where the tent stood. Men were busy putting up folding chairs, turning hay bales and planks into benches for tables, setting out literature, and stringing banners. Nearby, other workmen were building a stage and rolling a huge electrical generator into place. An Air National Guard helicopter sat poised for medical emergencies.

Game wardens, state wildlife biologists, and the U.S. Fish and Wildlife Service prepared for the big to-do. I milled around watching, finally deciding to pitch in when guilt got the better of me. (I was raised as a Catholic.) In an hour, the preparations were finished.

As the trucks started to rumble away down the dusty roads, I strolled to the south side of the hill and surveyed the scene. The Chase Lake dedication came at a crucial time—and in a very appropriate place. Below me lay a pothole, one of the millions that had at one time pocked the prairie. Trading in and out, over a low rise, were small flocks of ducks working their way back to the large lake on the nearby Chase Lake National Wildlife Refuge. That low rise has been known for many years as Chase Lake Pass, a historic spot for duck hunters of another era. The birds now on the lake were some of the few that had managed to survive this drought year; perhaps they had even raised an unlikely brood. Gathering now in the last week in September, they were preparing for the day when they would venture south.

There was a time within the memory of living men when a hunter could sit at Chase Lake Pass and shoot ducks at will. When the prairie ecosystem was intact, ducks prospered here. And when local flocks showed migrating birds the pattern over that rise, combining the flocks, a person sitting in that spot could see the October skies turned black with ducks. The heavens were torn with the gasp of set wings, hushed by the whispered whistle of air through pinions. Over the vast, lush prairie ducks of every type traded.

The sight is gone now, the flights of birds mere memories. Some formerly abundant species are now rare blessings for the watchful. A hunter might still shoot a duck here, but he had better be armed with more patience than shotgun shells.

When I looked to the north, I easily saw the answer to why the waterfowl had disappeared. Acres of wheat mixed with rows of corn spanned the landscape. What land wasn't plowed was grazed, sometimes heavily. Dust was part of the harvest.

Drought, machinery, diligence, and hard work had simply left no place for ducks.

The dedication was beginning. Rascal and I broke camp and drove to a spot a few miles to the north. Tour buses filled with participants lined the road, and someone's pasture had been turned into a parking lot. Volunteers waved arms and directed traffic.

Perhaps two hundred people milled on the prairie. Banners snapped in the stiff wind, as did the flags of the United States, Canada, Mexico, and North Dakota. Television crews were poking lenses into everything, looking for ten seconds' worth of film for the evening news. I wasn't sure that all the activity would help to convince the farmers that they could raise a

The Chase Lake Project

Located just north and west of Jamestown, North Dakota, the Chase Lake Project is an ambitious plan to restore habitat necessary to prairie-nesting waterfowl and other wildlife. As the flagship of the North American Waterfowl Management Plan (NAWMP) on the American prairie, the project is looking for ways to make the land both profitable for agriculture and habitable by wildlife. The NAWMP calls for restoration of the continental fall flight of ducks to one hundred million birds from the 1989–90 levels of sixty million. The last time such numbers were reached was in the early 1970s.

The 4,385-acre Chase Lake National Wildlife Refuge is in the heart of the project. Initially work will be done in a core area around the refuge, encompassing 335 square miles. The Chase Lake Project plan calls for the effort to expand into an additional 8,600 square miles of North Dakota prairie by the year 2000.

The major goals of the plan are to raise the region's duck production by 300 percent and to protect significant habitats of all types of ground-nesting prairie birds, including some threatened species.

The project calls for landowner participation to be stimulated through financial incentives and education. Nesting structures, predator fencing, delayed haying, rotational grazing, land acquisition and easements, reduced use of pesticides, and restoration of wetlands will all be tools used to restore the diversity and quantity of habitat and wildlife.

Most of the work will be done on privately owned lands. An interpretive center for prairie ecology and wildlife may eventually be built near the town of Medina.

heritage of wildlife as well as wheat. After all, farmers were practical and here, on the wide plains, very independent.

I wandered around during the ceremony. Straddling a ruined wetland were two groups of people. On the west was a podium and the attending dignitaries: the governor, representatives from the conservation agencies, and some local movers and shakers.

I turned with my back to the wind and stood behind the banners and podium, listening to the enthusiastic speeches being made. The flags snapped smartly in the gusts. It was easy to get caught up in the occasion, easy to wish that the hopes for the future would come true. Everyone spoke optimistically of the great benefits that would be derived from the implementation of the plan.

Then my gaze narrowed to the crowd on the east side of the drained pothole. These were the people—fewer than two hundred—who would determine whether or not wildlife would ever again live on their land.

I watched tall fathers with hands on children's shoulders and mothers clutching toddlers. Seed-company hats were pulled down firmly against the wind. The landowners listened attentively, or at least politely. What was going through their minds? Could they be convinced?

The speeches ended and everyone edged toward the ruined wetland. Hands rummaged in pockets and purses, retrieving small glass vials with black plastic caps. The vials were filled with earth, black North Dakota soil.

Into the ditch that some farmer on some forgotten blue sky prairie day had dug to drain this pothole the earth from the vials was liberated. I watched as the farmers and dignitaries each poured soil into the ditch that had emptied this pothole. A young father squatted next to a little boy of about four. He put the vial into the child's hand and together they emptied it into the ditch. The gesture was meaningful.

A big Cat fired up and rumbled down the slope. Sharp blade piling earth before it, the machine quickly moved enough Dakota soil into the gap to fill it. The pothole now would simply wait—wait for the drought to break, for the rain and snow to fill it, for the vegetation to grow, and for the ducks to return. I hoped it would be soon.

––––––––––––––––

Darkness that only comes to places far removed from cities enveloped the prairie. Standing outside my camper, beneath my lone tree, I looked up at the stars that blazed so brightly. If I climbed my tree I might touch them. But that night, despite the dedication of the wildlife managers and the obvious support of some landowners earlier in the day, I felt a nagging doubt about what I had seen. Throughout the tours and during the cook-out I had eavesdropped on conversations laced with resentment and skepticism, and even anger. These were natural reactions, I supposed, for good people who have been told that their hard work and productivity are part of the reason that this planet is in trouble.

Before the day had ended, Paul, a pilot for the state, had asked me if I'd like an airplane ride. In the little two-seater we sailed over the one-time prairie, and the true nature of the land became evident. Crossing the boundary from the refuge to farmland was like passing from the Serengeti to the Sahara. In the refuge, despite even the drought, there was water and wildlife. Deer jumped up from beds in bullrushes. Geese, ducks, swans, cranes, pelicans, and shorebirds of many kinds lounged in the relative lushness. On the other side of the fence, the earth was generally bare or interspersed with thin rows of leftover wheat stubble. Aside from some acres already enrolled in conservation programs, the farmland was a place where only man and his plant minions could live.

From this aerial perspective, it was very easy to see that although "prairie" was still used commonly to describe the countryside, the term had lost its original meaning. There were no acres of native plants, no herds of wild animals, no unaffected wetlands. Instead there lay a patchwork of roads, farmyards, and crops. Crops that no doubt were a thing of beauty to some but which had utterly changed the face of this part of the planet.

Seeing that impact that farming had made I wondered if the damage could ever be even partially reversed. I wondered if there were enough humility among people, enough generosity of spirit, and enough political fortitude to make the tough choices that would make the prairie live again. I could only hope there was.

SASKATCHEWAN

Saskatchewan is windy. Summer hasn't left the prairie, even on the twenty-seventh of September. The heat pours across the parking-lot-flat province as if someone had opened an immense oven door. I am hot, the dog is hot, and the wind rips from the northwest at what must be forty miles an hour.

You can't appreciate such a wind unless you've driven a pick-up truck with a camper straight into it. Even though my camper is the type that cranks up, it still catches the wind, and I feel as though I am driving with a parachute billowed out behind me. The road here runs northwest into the teeth of the wind.

Canada uses the metric system, and I strain my brain trying to compute kilometers into miles until I realize that the speedometer in the truck also shows kilometers per hour. But there's no need to worry about breaking the speed limit with this wind. My foot mashes the gas pedal, but I feel as though I am barely moving.

Having left Chase Lake at sunrise, I'm anxious to reach Regina. The rolling hills (hill is a relative term on the plains) of the Missouri Coteau guided me north and west, past Minot and through the Des Lacs River valley.

The Souris River runs through this country. You can't see it from the road except where you cross it. In one farmyard along the highway stands a hand painted sign: "Damn the Wildlife. Dam the Souris. Support the Water Project." Here is a farmer with priorities.

This part of Saskatchewan is so flat that it seems I can see for a million miles. From what I can tell, there is not one acre that has not felt the hand of man. Though people are few and far between, the land has been altered so much that there is no place where one can walk amongst nature, where one can see or feel anything of the true prairie. Like the hot wind that presses against the truck, man's heavy hand weighs down the land.

As we speed toward Regina, I see only wheat fields, dirt roads, farmhouses and outbuildings. Even a field mouse would have a hard time living here, for only the roadside ditches have grass.

Somewhere near Lang, I pull off the road and let Rascal run in the seared grass of a ditch. Grasshoppers flush. A fine dust covers everything. I feel it on my skin and on my sweaty neck. My eyeglasses are coated with a thin film of dust. So are my lips. The dust tastes slightly alkaline.

While Rascal rummages in the grass, I go to the back of the truck and open the camper. Cold Lake Superior water tastes good; I fill the dog's dish, too. I will ration this carefully. Knowing that water in the prairies is not generally good, I filled the camper tank and every water jug I owned before leaving Duluth. I grab two cold beers before Rascal and I get back into the truck for the last push into the hot wind.

"Warning—Private Road, Travel at Your Own Risk." What a strange sign to see in the middle of nowhere. I stopped the truck. It could have meant that the road was in bad shape. Or what it might have referred to, but I could hardly believe it, was that I was entering Indian Reserve 88, that mere pink blotch on my road map. More than once I had been warned recently, under the breath and with many glances around, about straying onto or camping near Indian reserves. I didn't want to believe it.

As a precaution, I turned the truck around. I hadn't really wanted to come this way in the first place but had been detoured by road construction. Now, lost in the middle of the Touchwood Hills, I pulled to the side of the road, having put a mile between me and the sign before digging out the map.

I was more than five hundred miles from Chase Lake and more than one hundred miles north of Regina. As I headed for the Quill Lakes area, I traveled through undulating, aspen covered highlands. I had expected cooler weather but even now the drought hung on, the heat rising in the shimmering waves off the road surface. For two days Rascal had ridden with her black, block head on my leg or arm, content but obviously hoping for more than just a long drive.

I, too, wanted more. I wanted to feel the urgency of the pending winter, to see the waterfowl migration in its splendor. But I was still driving north, not south with the birds, and summer wouldn't loosen its grip. Although the stop at Chase Lake had revealed some birds, what I had seen most since leaving home was wheat. And instead of listening to goose music, I had heard the depressed tones of wildlife managers, who were worried about the future of prairie wildlife.

Rascal and I had stayed the previous night in a motel on the outskirts of Regina, a silver city rising from the province's wheat wealth. I had then

spent the morning talking to Ducks Unlimited biologists and wildlife managers for the province—folks who were working to save ducks. In their
voices were both despair and hope. I was left with two feelings: that the
waterfowl (read that "wetlands") crisis is probably worse than most of us can
imagine, and that I wanted to get out of the city to see ducks and geese, to
see the wetlands and farms. I am a doubting Thomas. I had to put my hand
in the wound.

I didn't have to travel far. These upland hills of Saskatchewan contain
many of the last intact wetlands in the province. Unlike the easily drained
prairie potholes, these wetlands are surrounded by a stunted, twisted aspen
forest and therefore were low on the list for development (a term used
positively by some but which, in my dictionary, falls perilously close to the
word *destruction*). The Touchwood Hills are where the prairie petered out
and ran headlong into the ancient forest that for centuries had been creeping down from the arctic, its growth once checked only by fire. But today I
watched as farmers sheared the hills, plowing the trees into the potholes,
destroying forest and water in one fell swoop, leaving great mounds of
aspen corpses contorted in wet graves. What water was left was rimmed
with black earth; a duck returning here to nest might just as well set down
in a rain puddle in a parking lot.

To continue my search for some place where the cycle that had evolved
over eons still took place unchecked, I pulled ahead and began to look for a
road heading north. A cloud of dust on an intersecting road materialized
into a Royal Canadian Mounted Police squad car. I waved my arm, and the
car stopped. The officer cautiously rolled her window down as I pulled
alongside to ask directions. A weathered old man, an Indian with deep
fissures in his leathery face, smiled at me from the backseat of the squad car.
He appeared to be handcuffed. He was very, very drunk. He was telling
himself some immensely funny jokes and then chortling. The old man's
dark eyes were warm and watery, very sad and yet unconcerned in his
alcohol-induced euphoria. I wanted to ask why he was being arrested, but
checked myself. Drunkenness was probably reason enough.

After thanking the Mountie, I moved on. My map showed the big blue
butterfly of the Quill Lakes, just to the north. I had directions and would
find my way. Maybe I would also find ducks.

I turned on the tape deck. I felt very bad for the old Indian, felt very
bad for the ducks. Both had been pushed into a corner. It would be easier
not to think about either.

I sank slowly down onto a rock. Rascal hunkered nearby, trying to hide behind a scraggly bush. The tripod with the camera and big lens was in front of me, and another camera hung around my neck on a strap. We were just on the water's edge.

Blue sky gave way to violet then to black from the horizon skyward as the watery yellow sun set slowly. Only the slightest breeze blew from the northwest, hardly enough movement to raise a ripple on the small lake but cooling anyway. My feet made small, muddy impressions on the lake's edge. "It's a treat to beat your feet on the Saskatchewanian mud."

A few geese sang their way from the wheat fields to the north, squawking merrily in the early evening, bellies full. Ten or twelve white-fronted geese swung by and looked right at us. I could see their long necks twist our way as the camera's motor drive whirred. The geese circled the lake until they found a place that they liked, that would look the same as any other place on the small lake to you or me but that they found different and better, and so they cranked down their landing gear, cupped their wings, and slowly settled down, splayed yellow webbing hissing on the water.

The sky glowed orange now, and the few clouds looked like smoky wisps against its brilliance. Maybe the ducks would come. A yellowleg sandpiper skimmed the water in front of us and gracefully dropped its spindly legs and landed in the shallows in front of Rascal. Ears up, the dog quivered and looked at me as if to say "I can catch this one, boss. Puhleease!" I told her to stay.

Usually the wind dies with the sun but now it picked up its pace slightly, coming cold from a place where the frost never really leaves the ground. It felt good, after the days of heat and the dryness of these prairies, to be chilled and have water lapping at my feet and birds in the air. Finally.

There was half an hour of light left, fifteen minutes of which would be suitable for photography. As if on cue, more geese honked high in the almost clear sky, but they were hard to see against the coming darkness. Thinly they talked. Within minutes, though, the birds were near enough for me to identify them. Their talking told us of them. Canada geese first, then snows.

The geese started down, backlit against the setting sun. I peered through the viewfinder and shot them.

I waited for the flock to end. It didn't. From their arctic nesting grounds they came, tired and thirsty. First mama gathering her brood, then broods gathering to flocks, now flocks gathering into a raucous mass. The summer was over. The first snows had come. Fly to where the summer still is! Fly to food and water.

The lake beckoned, and the specks called. Undulating in the smoky orange sky the sinuous black flocks met and joined and I could see there was no end to them. This was not just a feeding flock coming in to rest for the night, bellies and crops full of waste wheat from harvested fields. This was a major migration, and I was here with them. The air was full with their song, the *ker-rhonk, ker-rhonk* of the Canadas and the barking of the snows. As far to the north as I could see there were geese.

I took photographs until it was too dark to shoot anymore. Rascal trembled in the cold wind—but not from the chill. Long after the beginning of the flock had passed (most of the birds seemed bent on heading to Little Quill Lake, a mile to the south), geese still came in an unbroken string. A half hour passed. So did ten thousand geese. Small groups would drop out, swing right over us to circle the lake, and then, with no small degree of fanfare and what sounded to me like happiness and relief, would set down on the little lake, dipping, tipping, leaves in a gust, first on the far shore, then, as the lake filled and the darkness hid me better, nearer and nearer.

Five or six ducks came in low and landed. That was all.

———————————

I don't suppose that, if you have never sat in a duck blind or a goose pit, you can possibly know what it is like to see the world come alive in the morning and have it all embodied by the birds. I also don't suppose you can then understand why it is that we hunters would shoot these birds that we so admire. And then, it follows that I probably won't be able to adequately describe why we do what we do or how it feels and sounds and tastes to do it. If the thought of it all offends you, then take this book back to the store now, before you crinkle the cover or leave thumbprints on the pages, and get your money back. If you would like to know a little bit about it all, then read on. I don't guarantee anything though.

Autumn mornings are cold, and when you need to use bare hands to place the decoys and build blinds, they quickly become numb even though the rest of your overdressed body is sweaty from exertion. Most of these preparations are made while it is still dark so that in the first mauve moments of light you can be sitting in your blind and sipping coffee. Many goose hunters dig pits in which to hide on the otherwise barren landscape.

I had found a squadron of geese feeding in a wheat field the day before that sunset and spotted what I thought was an enormous stroke of good fortune—a lone willow bush that had been left standing on the edge of the field. Rascal and I now sat in its cover.

In front of this willow bush were about four dozen field shells, or legless goose decoys, mounted on stakes. (You can arrange these fakes to look much like a group of feeding birds.) The decoys were placed in a stubble field of wheat—wheat chopped off about six inches above the ground so that the entire field, in the morning light and from ground level, looked as though it had a butch haircut. My mother always "mowed" my hair the day after school was out so that she could more easily scrub me clean.

There you have it. A man and a dog sitting in a bush, in the almost-pitch-black, someplace on the globe, a small place, two creatures, the immenseness of the planet sweeping away from them, hoping that by luck or skill they have guessed at being in just the same place, for just a few seconds, as geese, who have only recently come from a half a continent away. Talk about optimism.

My truck is hidden (sort of) behind some aspen trees. There is a shotgun, still unloaded, propped next to me as I squirm on a folding stool, warming my frozen fingers around a steaming cup of coffee.

The great Quill Lakes, big saline bodies of water that for eons have been a major staging area for waterfowl gathering for migration, lie about half a mile right in front of us. Stubble stretches nearly to water's edge in front of us, and well behind us, broken here and there by patches of aspen trees and scrubby willow.

One by one the stars to the east wink out. A narrow band of light shows along the horizon, outlining the few trees. I wiggle my toes in my boots to keep them warm. Rascal has rime on the whiskers nearest her nose.

Still not two years old, Rascal has never hunted geese but is taut with anticipation. A small songbird, unidentifiable in the darkness, flits within inches of her head, and she comes nearly unglued. Chuckling, I tell her, "Stay," and run my hand down her slick neck, feeling her excitement surface.

Because a slight wind comes from the west (our right), I expect the geese to come from the east, at least when approaching the decoys. They, like airplanes, land into the wind, so waterfowlers always try to set up with the wind at their backs or, at the very least (as on this occasion), quartering. Finally, it is light enough to make out the decoys, especially the white snow-geese ones, and I grab the shotgun and practice rising to shoot. I discover I'll have to step forward, then up, to avoid the willow branches that hide us.

Rascal growls and looks to the right. I watch her, using her muzzle as a pointer, then look where she looks. She rumbles.

Drifting from the tall grass on the edge of the stubble flows a tawny form. I put a restraining hand on Rascal's collar. The sun breaks above the horizon, lighting the creeping thing. It is a coyote, head low, butt up, tail pluming, stalking our decoys. Of course, it doesn't know that these aren't geese, but thinks instead of its incredible good fortune. Each paw moves ever so slowly. Complete stop. The coyote senses something is amiss. But its stomach tries to deny it. The stomach sees, wants, blood, meat, feathers flying. A coyote has no qualms about killing. It is its job. It is good at it. It is beautiful.

Watching this creature slink stealthily, I admire it, even feel akin to it. We are both hunters, have been for all the time of our species. I also see Rascal in that coyote, the coyote in Rascal. Not much time or evolution or breeding even separates them. Her fire is quick to erupt, nearer the surface than mine, but still related.

Rascal barks, startling me. Her bark comes as a surprise even to her, and I laugh at the shocked look on her face. The coyote, maybe twenty yards away, is so confused that it jumps backward, takes a wide path around the decoys through the amber field, and lopes east—the whole time looking over its shoulder at the barking bush.

I cheer the rising sun because I am cold, even though I know that geese fly nearer the ground on cloudy days. I check my watch to make sure it is legal to shoot. I rummage in my pocket for shotgun shells. The first one clunks into the chamber of the old Browning shotgun, and I put two in the magazine. Goose hunting may be new to her, but Rascal knows what this is all about when she sees the shotgun readied and hears the bolt working.

Wings on the wind alert us. A flock of ducks, silent in flight except for the rustling of primaries, circles the field. I talk to them on the duck call, and a hen talks back. Soon we converse freely. Another pass is made. Wings set. The flock comes low. Mallards. Forty or so.

When they are in range, I stand up and start shooting, and I keep shooting until I have shot the entire flock. Then I sit down and put my camera away. Rascal is confused, but I have honored my self-imposed limit on ducks. I will shoot few on this long journey, picking always the drakes and leaving the hens to return to the far-flung marshes to breed, killing just enough to satisfy my soul, my hunger. Today I will use my gun only on geese, because their populations are healthy and growing.

Across the stubble, from beyond the trees comes the sound of geese: the barking snows, the honking Canadas, and the tootling white-fronts. The stubble is amber, the aspens, gold. It is a butterscotch morning under the slanting prairie sun. My left cheek is warmed by the rising sun, but the back of my neck is still cold where it faces the night. Sounding for all the world like the Indian war whoops of a low-budget cowboy movie, the geese come in waves, circling above the aspens to feel the wind and then strike off to the north to feed. I have guessed correctly: they will come our way.

I have heard timber wolves howl, loons sing, the bellowing grunt of a bull moose in rut. These are wonderful sounds. Nothing, though, compares to the thrill of goose music, for it is at once joyous and wild, raucous and serene. Maybe the sound of bluebills, their wings ripping the wind as they drop en masse from the sky, comes near. But it is quick, and startling, and over in seconds. Goose song comes slowly, building, and like a symphony, reaches a crescendo, the cacophony filling the sky and the soul as they pass overhead. Every human cell remembers the sound from an era when seasons were measured in the comings and goings of waterfowl.

Hordes of geese are coming, flocks merging and splitting, yet all working north. The first group passes to my right, low enough but too wide. This is a bad sign, because although they leave no tracks in the sky, flock follows flock. In moments, a thousand geese have ignored my decoys.

Watching these in the distance, I hear others near. A low-flying flock of snow geese is heading for the decoys. If they had remained silent, they might have escaped, for like people, geese might stay out of trouble by keeping their mouths shut. The leader is craning its neck. It seems the decoys look good, and I am doing my best to beckon them in on the goose call, playing gleefully.

Wings cup. Rascal trembles. I tremble, too. Our hearts quicken. There is nothing but me, the dog, the geese, the vast prairie sky, and a horizon that stretches to the distant past. The rest of the world disappears. All at once I see great beauty, hear, taste, smell wind, wings, dust, feathers, fur, gun smoke. These are memories, realities, rolled into one, woven from many. It is my present, my past, my race's past. It is the same for the geese, the dog.

I drop the goose call and slowly pick up the shotgun. I whisper, "Stay," to the dog. They have come.

I remember to step forward, then up. Over the gun barrel I see startled geese rowing wildly for altitude, pick out one white bird, squeeze the trigger. *Whump.* The gun kicks, but I do not feel the jolt as I swing the gun onto, then past, a second bird as the first one tumbles. *Whump.* The gun belches. *Whump,* again. Then the flock is gone.

The second goose is dead, the first is only injured. I point it out to Rascal. I needn't have. Chestnut eyes are boring a path to it, waiting. I softly say, "Back."

Dust flies. Rascal streaks through the stubble and leaps over a decoy. The goose, seeing the dog, rears up to face her, face death. Rascal bowls the big snow over, turns to pick it up, and is soundly struck across her head with a wing. The goose hisses. Rascal studies this bird, the largest she has ever seen, hesitates for a second and then, with a quick lunge, is inside the beating wings, clamping her mouth around it. Her head high, she proudly carries the heavy load back, one wing across her face. She carefully puts the bird in my hand. Solemnly, averting my eyes from those of the goose, I wring its neck.

My goose is a beautiful goose, a brilliant white mature snow with glossy black wing-tips. I try to span the broad chest with my hand but can't. I spread the black-and-white wings—wings that have passed over a continent—to their full seventeen inches. The legs and bill are pink—legs that have waddled across tundra, a bill that has grazed the arctic. When I gently lay the bird on the ground, Rascal stoops and sniffs. I sit her down, point out the second bird, and send her to retrieve it.

I am very happy but also a little sad. Then from the south I hear geese honking. Rascal and I dive into the bush. She moves to our geese and sits next to them, touching them.

The geese are coming.

The tiny woman brought the tray of drinks to our table; three people, six glasses. I had ordered a scotch-and-soda and so got a scotch and a soda. Canadian law said I had to mix them myself.

Ross Melinchuk and Nolan Matthies had two glasses apiece. Rum in one, Coca Cola (I believe) in the other. We mix our drinks, and sip. At this late hour, we are almost alone in a restaurant in Wynyard, south of the Quills. We discuss the coming morning's goose hunt and the plight of the ducks. Only the thought of the hunt tempers my despair over the ducks.

"Let me tell you this," said Ross. "The situation is bad and the stakes are big. Make no mistake about it. This is our last chance to save the ducks. If we lose this battle, that's it. We won't have another chance.

"Actually, the drought, agriculture, everything that has brought the ducks to crisis has at least had the positive effect of bringing the situation into focus. And to people beyond just the duck hunters, who have always fought for wetlands," he continued. "That's what this is. A battle to save wetlands and all the life that depends upon them, not just ducks. Ducks are just a way to measure it all, the 'canary in the mineshaft.'"

In this age of environmentalism, there are a lot of "canaries in mineshafts," an analogy with the birds that were used by miners to test air quality deep underground. Sick or dead birds meant sick or dead miners. Simple. And profound. What is good for animals is also good for man. Clean water, clean air—those things that life depends upon are nearly constant. And so we have spotted owls that are the test for Pacific coast old growth forests, and eagles and ospreys testing the food chain for dangerous pesticides and toxins. Now we see ducks as indicators of wetland abundance or health. So simple. It is handwriting on the wall for a society that is apparently largely illiterate.

Despite the enormous task of overseeing the largest waterfowl project in North America under the guidelines of the North American Waterfowl Management Plan, Ross is optimistic. By the year 2000, the goal is to restore waterfowl to the levels of the early 1970s, the last time they reached anything resembling their historic numbers. He digs into his food, talking all the while. He is proud of the work done on the Quill Lakes Project, the ambitious plan to restore duck populations and wetlands on the Saskatchewan prairie and uplands.

I watch him. Young, dark, and bearded, he is full of enthusiasm. The challenge excites him. It is an opportunity that few biologists get a chance at, for he is at a crossroads and can be a major player, can actually turn the tide. Or sink in it. He knows it. And I think to myself, "How can we lose with people like him fighting?" It is easy to like him.

I think back to earlier in the day, when we toured the area in Ross's

Ducks, Drought, and Agriculture

Ducks have evolved around drought. In dry years the birds retreat to more-permanent bodies of water, awaiting the eventual reflooding of their favored prairie potholes. They may breed little in those dry years, but because they are relatively long-lived and capable of hatching large broods when optimal conditions return, ducks have historically been able to rebound quickly from drought.

In recent times, however, droughts have been devastating to ducks. Although prairie wetlands benefit from drought and are usually more productive after drought has recycled their nutrients, the advent of intensive agriculture on the prairie has led to the converting of wetlands to cropland during drought years. During a drought, thousands of potholes are ditched, drained, and plowed. They are then severely degraded as wildlife habitat, or gone forever.

Suburban, traveling dusty roads on a drought-drenched prairie. Ross recited the litany, a sad litany that was strikingly similar to what I had heard during my stop in North Dakota. How in the hell can he be so optimistic?

"Look," he said, "this section here is part of the 8,000 acres of land we've purchased. Next year it will be seeded to dense nesting cover."

Later, pointing out heavy machinery digging a trench, "This water-control project will allow us to keep these wetlands flooded."

These successes are his cause for optimism, because they represent the cooperation of local farmers. This is the key, he explained. We'll always have droughts. The destruction of potholes and uplands are the factors that are limiting production—of ducks, prairie grouse, songbirds, wading birds. The whole issue, then, revolves around a simple equation: more upland cover near undisturbed wetlands equals more wildlife.

There are other benefits as well. Marshlands act as reservoirs; they

In Saskatchewan, which provides 34 percent of the continent's mallards, an estimated historical number of five million mallards had been reduced to a million or less by 1989, due primarily to agricultural practices.

Agriculture also affects prairie-nesting birds, such as waterfowl, by removing the natural prairie's dense nesting cover on the uplands. Ducks need more than water to successfully reproduce. Some species may nest in tall, dense grass, as far as a mile from the nearest wetland. Most of this nesting cover has been converted to cropland. The narrow margin of nesting cover left unfarmed around the perimeter of a wetland often becomes a death trap by concentrating birds and predators into the same habitat.

Numbers of predators, such as skunks, crows, foxes, and raccoons, have increased across the prairie as agriculture makes the landscape more hospitable to them. The lack of nesting cover for ducks has meant easy hunting for the predators in the remaining small patches of habitat. In some regions, nesting success is at or below 10 percent, and many hens have had to renest just to attain that low figure. Twenty percent success is necessary just to maintain most duck species' numbers.

retard flooding, recharge groundwater, help maintain soil moisture, and function as natural purifiers to break down farming residues. Storing water where it is needed most and is the most efficient, wetlands can actually increase farm production: the stored soil moisture offsets any loss of acreage that might have been gained by drainage and conversion to croplands. Given financial incentives, area farmers were very receptive to participating in programs that would result in preserving the land.

A job, I thought to myself, they ought to be doing anyway. After all, the one thing a farmer can't buy when it wears out is good, moist, erosion-free soil. We continued our tour until dark, the vastness of the prairie night engulfing us until the truck was really only a tiny pinprick of light bobbing along the trails, hardly worth a second look, making me feel very small.

A groan or two brings me back to the present. Each of us pushes back from the table, stuffed with bamboo shoots, rice, peapods, and the like.

Nolan, who, like Ross, works for the Saskatchewan Department of Parks, Recreation, and Culture, and is Director of Communications, lights up a cigarette.

He says, "The work that is being done here is tremendously important, and not just to the hunter. Everyone benefits from clean water, more wildlife, and a generally healthier environment."

Ross and I nod in agreement. Why, then, is it so damn hard to convince most people?

Pounding, pounding, then a voice: "Are you up in there? Time to go goose hunting," Ross said from behind the motel door. Four o'clock. Jesus. I was hardly awake, and he was already outside at the trucks. I jumped out of bed and dressed madly.

And so the three of us were on our way from Wynyard, south of the Quills, to Wadena, in the northeast, to meet Randy, Ross's goose-guide friend. I followed the speeding red taillights of Ross's rig down the smooth Saskatchewan highway in the last half of the black night. In Wadena we transferred our gear to Randy's truck. Rascal, unfortunately, stayed behind in my rig.

It was still dark, and inside the truck I was unable to see the stars. I became miserably turned around as we drove down this and then that country road, finally to bounce across stubble fields. Ross and Randy chatted about where geese had been spotted recently. Nolan seemed incredibly good humored for such an early hour. I missed my morning coffee very badly. When we stopped, I had no idea where we were—although, most likely, we were still in Saskatchewan.

Goose hunting is not easy work. Setting out a big spread of decoys takes time, and then a place to hide must be prepared. On this dark morning we raked three piles of wheat straw into neat heaps, made small nests inside each, and then lay back, our heads supported by shell bags or rolled-up jackets, shotguns lying at our sides. Finally, we covered ourselves with the remaining straw.

When you are as bundled up as a child sent out to play in January in Minnesota and are lying on your back staring into the black prairie sky, counting stars you never knew existed, all is right. No one but a hunter is crazy enough to do this, so no one but a hunter knows how it feels: cold, prickly, invigorating, exciting, calming—and it smells damn good. You can almost fall asleep, as I did.

Then, all of a sudden, the pile of hay nearest me spoke. "It's time," Ross said. "Look east."

I did, and saw in the sunrise a swarm of geese rising from its night roost, a wisp of black smoke twisting noisily into the morning sky, in flux, never the same, flowing.

Despite our efforts at calling and our concealment, no geese were tempted to come near. Thousands flew by, but never in range. They are smart, these geese.

Finally, as we were about to quit, cold and cramped, with a purple storm front approaching from the north and pushing the pillowed white clouds from its path, and the morning sun, then maybe about eight o'clock low, beaming across the wheat stubble and turning aspen stands from black to gold, a small flock of Canada geese came low from the east. Ross saw them first and cried out. They never uttered a sound.

We dived into our hay piles, fussing briefly. The dark geese sashayed right up to the decoy spread, and came down. Wondering at their size, I almost forgot to shoot. I was nearest to them.

Ross, thinking I'd gone daft, shouted to me. "Mike, now!"

I sat up and pointed the gun at one big honker only ten yards up. When the gun spoke, the bird tumbled. Then the rest of the flock vanished. Poof. Gone.

Ross ran to pick up the goose and studied it as he lugged it over to me. Held by its neck and level with Ross's shoulder, the big bird hung nearly to the ground. Ross's was not the look of a biologist studying a specimen. His was the look of love, respect.

"Awfully nice bird, Mike," he said, setting it down in the clean straw. "This is one of the big Canadas."

We packed up and went to breakfast. Everyone else went to work, while I, reunited with Rascal, drove into the countryside to camp and pluck—which is how I found the feeding snow geese and the lone willow bush and the dandy camping place beneath the golden aspens and the little lake where I would see the ten thousand geese at sunset. I would spend nearly a week here.

I don't know if it is because Americans have a different look about them or because in the small towns I visited anyone new would be obvious (Wynyard has about 2,500 souls, Wadena, 1,500) but I felt like a nudist in a Baptist church. Sitting in a restaurant was interesting. The local Saskatchewanians would stare, averting their eyes when caught. Except the old women. They'd stare you down, and if you smiled they would turn to a crony, say something, and then they would all look at you. But none of them returned your smile.

One man, drunk at ten in the morning, weaved on the curb in front of the old Wadena Hotel, where I had breakfast one day after hunting. After seeing my truck and its Minnesota plates, he said, "Damn those Yanks and their crop subsidies. They're really screwing us. Why don't they stay at home?" I walked away as someone tried to hush him.

One night in the camper, as I cooked a late supper of mallard breasts, sauteed in bacon drippings, steamed in dry wine with crumbled bacon, fried onions, and a dollop of orange marmalade on top of each, a strange little man came to the camper door. It was pitch dark, and I watched as his flashlight beam bobbed to the camper. I was staying in a tiny campground near the nearly nonexistent town of Clair, and he explained, as we spoke through the door (after Rascal growled at him, he wouldn't come in and glanced cautiously at the dog as we spoke), that he was collecting the camping fee. He loosened up as we spoke and finally let loose a twenty-minute torrent of political frustration. The damn Tories, he said, were making a mess of Saskatchewan. Only the wealthy could exist. Hated them, hated the mess, and was thinking of moving.

"Where?" I queried.

"Alberta."

I was stumped. He made it sound like Alberta was a foreign country. Wouldn't there be Tories in Alberta too?

"Oh, they don't like Tories in Alberta. It's a much more sensible place than Saskatchewan, eh?"

Who am I to argue?

Despite the way they stared at me, the people were extremely courteous on the road. Try this in Saskatchewan sometime. Pull up to someone's bumper on the highway. The driver of the car ahead immediately swerves over onto the shoulder! He actually lets you pass! The first time this happened, I almost came to a stop. I thought the other car had blown a tire because it moved sideways so quickly.

Prairie farmers seemed oblivious to the grand spectacle of ducks and geese. Time after time, as I toured the area, I would screech to a halt just to take in the spectacle of geese and cranes. Just as frequently, I'd watch a farmer work on, immune, it seems, to the same spectacle.

I cannot tell you adequately just what wildlife does for the feel of the prairie. The works of man here in Saskatchewan are roads, grain elevators (big, white, towering structures with POOL written in huge letters on their sides), railroad tracks, houses, barns, and farm fields. At this time of year the fields are being plowed after harvest, so by winter they are gigantic, barren, black, dust-seething wastelands. Deserts.

Step aside and find an untouched piece of native prairie or marshland, and the entire landscape takes on a different perspective. The same rich organic and slightly alkaline soil that so readily grows wheat pushes up a diverse population of grass and forbs. Flowers are abundant, and because the land has not been poisoned with herbicides and pesticides, the eco-system, from the bottom up, exists. Insects. Mice. Rabbits. And so on until you come to the predators, both mammal and avian. So, too, the wetlands are bountifully alive, their lavishness standing in stark contrast to the surrounding farmlands. Shorebirds *peent–peent–peent* when you startle them; mallards leap skyward, wings pounding air; and muskrats munch contentedly on cattails, their chewing an audible rasping in the marsh. Birds, fish, mammals, flowers, grasses, reeds, insects—the prairie and adjacent wetlands live. And the waterfowl are their most magical voice.

Without waterfowl, autumn in the agricultural prairie would be merely three months of dust, a long wait for sparse snowfall. Not only the season's definition, not only a timeless timekeeper, the migrating waterfowl make the prairie come alive.

Trilling call, electric by nature, wafted over the yellow aspens. Drifting effortlessly on wings seven feet wide, gangly legs trailing, the sandhill cranes arrived from the tundra. The dwarf trees of the taiga were behind them. Wings had swept them over the shifting herds of caribou. Winds had blown them past countless lakes and brawling rivers, white and black rents on the landscape. Finally the northern forests had dwindled and were met by the prairie, where the great masses of cranes could pause and feed on their way to the wintering grounds of Texas and Mexico. The sparse stubble field awaited them. Lifting their wings up and throwing their spindly legs forward and down, the great gray birds parachuted to the earth and began to feed.

I had never seen cranes so near and these were particularly brave, not minding me as they strutted slowly, leaving their gigantic three-toed tracks in the soil. The mature adults sported deep-red foreheads, the immature birds were solidly brown. Deliberately, they grazed.

More electric *whrrttt–whrrttt*s came from the north, heralding another flock of sandhills passing low over the prairie. Ten or so came, wide wings flicking, barely clearing a weathered, abandoned farmhouse and a windmill that would never turn again.

As I watched that scene, so typical of the prairies and marshes, I wondered about the durability of nature. Here were signs of human failure. The cranes still came, but the family that had tried to survive in this place had disappeared, the only sign of their temporary hold on the land the soon-to-tumble buildings.

In the ancient rhythms of nature, in the vibrant music of cranes, I saw hope. I could feel the fleeting grasp of man in this farm's failure, feel the endurance of nature in this ancient return of the cranes.

The return of the cranes spoke something of their eternal faith, faith that what has always been will always be. They, loyal to that faith, return, dependent upon constancy. The cranes know nothing of our struggles. The cranes merely want their due: places to nest, to feed, to rest.

Rascal and I watched the cranes as we stood in the rutted prairie road. From the north came more cranes, carving lazy circles as they descended to their fellows. What had only minutes before been only a dusty field of wheat stubble was suddenly alive with waving rows of storklike birds marching to and fro on legs with knobby knees. When a thousand birds had come, we quietly backed the truck away from them. This spot belonged to the cranes.

Full night had come. The procession of geese continued into the darkness, and still they came—thousands and thousands. It was very cold and windy. Small waves lapped the shore near my feet. Stars blossomed, so tightly packed and so whitely shining that I almost felt pain in their coldness and in my relative insignificance.

A father and his two grown sons had moved into the little campground where I have been staying this week. They, like the majority of hunters who visit this region, were from Minnesota and Wisconsin, states with rich wetland and wildfowl traditions but now bereft of the both.

In his seventies, the father remembered the dark clouds of ducks. While Rascal played with his golden retriever, he talked longingly of his youth, when the Mississippi River between Minnesota and Wisconsin was alive with ducks. He recounted days spent in a skiff in the pungent marshes, with vast shadows of mallards sweeping down from the north. The birds had been so thick that he, with his skill, could pick out the big green-headed drakes and drop them from the sky, filling his limit with only prime specimens.

The old man had passed on this love of wildfowl to his sons who, by the unfortunate trick of being born too late, would never see what he saw. In the span of one man's life, the natural world had changed and the ducks were now truly shadows, not casting them. The thought that frightened me was that my generation, not knowing and sometimes even doubting the wonder of such huge migrations, might be satisfied with something less. And when we were gone would our progeny be satisfied with even less? Not knowing or loving this wild spectacle, would future generations be willing to make the sacrifices necessary to restore, or even to maintain, the ducks? Or would prairie birds go the way of prairie mammals, and, like the bison, be found only in biology books, a two-sentence statement that at one time they had been quite numerous?

Coyotes spoke back in the forest, yipping coldly. Rascal snapped to attention. Perhaps they had found the remains of the geese I had cleaned far back in the woods, geese that having flown south to escape the frigid arctic autumn now lay stiff in a commercial freezer in Wadena, waiting for me to pick them up when I left. I would ship them home to my wife, Mary Jo. They would get warm one last time, their brown skins crackling with goose and bacon fat in a hot oven. They would even come to the marshes again, with me, their atoms merged with mine.

I had experienced much on this trip to Saskatchewan. Melinchuk's enthusiasm buoyed me, and the endless wheat and fallow fields depressed me, especially the wind-blown topsoil that turned the air the color of smoke.

Later, Fred Thornton, a biologist for Ducks Unlimited, put the North American Waterfowl Management Plan and this Quill Lakes Project into perspective. "We're never going to be able to buy enough land to influence the situation. The Plan is about changing the landscape so that it can support both agriculture and wildlife. The major thing we should be trying to do is to keep more cover on the land. Then, I think, you'll truly see less black dirt in the springtime when ducks are flying around trying to find a nest site. If we can get everyone thinking this way, we might actually be able to pull this one from the fire."

I turned up my collar, zipped every zipper, and pulled down my cap. Growing even more chilled, I had nothing left to do but wander back to the camper. The day, which had started well before sunrise, had been long and lonely. I missed Mary Jo. Rascal, great company always, leaned against my leg in the black night. It was time to fold up the tripod and head for the sleeping bag.

As I stood to let the blood flow into my creaking legs, I listened to the night, heard the geese, now very much more subdued in the fastness, beneath the stars. Then I heard wings whistling. Ducks—the birds I had been waiting for and had seen so few of this week. Considering that this was one of the greatest staging areas in the world and that this might be the extent of their numbers was very scary.

I heard them pass from right to the left, swing low, and then set down, skidding to a stop on the lake not very far in front of us. A small flock, maybe a dozen. In the ebony hollow behind me I heard a voice. A mallard quacked coarsely, cynically.

Like most of my race, I turned my back on it and walked away.

MANITOBA

It is a long way from the Quills to Boissevain, Manitoba, especially if you detour through North Dakota, as I did. Leaving the big lakes, I traversed south (a tail wind at last) through Regina, backtracking my route north a week earlier. The prairies seemed even more desolate once I left the huge squadrons of geese behind.

I had chosen the route through North Dakota for one reason: United Parcel Service. I had a limit of frozen geese to ship home and found that in Canada no fast service was readily available. At a Canadian Postal Service office in Regina I had inquired about their express mail service.

"How long to get a package to Duluth, express mail?" I asked the bespectacled clerk.

Digging out a chart, he ran a finger to my home zip code. "At the earliest, seventy-two hours." I walked away wondering what the hell was express about *that*. I could drive the distance in twenty-four.

Instead, I decided to drive to Minot, North Dakota. I had worked hard to kill my geese, and I felt honor bound to make sure they arrived home in fit condition to eat. We rarely eat the meat of domesticated animals, preferring the flesh of those animals we harvest ourselves, feeling a sense of being a part of the food chain and relishing the leaner, chemical-free meat.

When I was done shipping the birds I prowled the freeways around Minot looking for a motel. Of greatest importance to me was price (cheap) and to Rascal, an open field for an evening run. We found both and the following morning we left for Manitoba.

You may wonder why after spending so much time in Saskatchewan I wanted to see another prairie province. Wouldn't they all be much the same? I couldn't answer that question and decided to find out. Additionally, I hoped to see some of the famous marshes I had heard about: the Minnedosa potholes and the fabled Delta and Oak Hammock marshes. Too, I wanted to see the great lakes of the north, Winnipeg and Manitoba, resting on the northeast boundaries of the great prairies. Beyond those reasons, I was just wandering, hoping to find something of interest.

Leaning into yet another strong north wind, the truck strained northward on Highway 83, past the sprawling Air Force base outside Minot, past the tiny towns of Ruthville and Lansford, until, suddenly, the road ran out and a sharp right turn put us on State Highway 5, heading east. The landscape here was much as I had been seeing, although this area did not have the characteristic aspen groves of the Quill Lakes region. Wheat was still king, and along the way I watched as farmers plowed the stubble under, preparing for winter and blowing their topsoil clear to Minnesota. One can't help but wonder why they do this, for their soil is what makes them rich. In the one hundred years that the white man has been farming in North America, he has lost half the topsoil that he found upon arrival. Apparently, American and Canadian farmers have at least this one thing in common.

There is, however, a striking difference between the two countries' wheat farms. Always, the farms in the United States looked more prosperous. Houses and barns were freshly painted, combines and other equipment shining next to the big pole buildings that have replaced barns. So often the Canadian farms looked dilapidated. I had mentioned this observation to a chance acquaintance in Saskatchewan, and he attributed it to the fact that in Canada if your farm looks profitable you'll get bumped into a higher tax bracket.

With a forty-mile-an-hour tail wind now, I flew toward the reed-banked Souris River, which flows through the J. Clark Salyer II National Wildlife Refuge. The river, green on a dusty day, looked inviting as Rascal and I slowed to a stop to watch as the ducks loafed along the west bank, protected from the seeking wind.

It was appropriate that the ducks were resting on this particular refuge. No one ever did as much for ducks as did J. Clark Salyer II. A dynamo of a biologist, he was in charge of spending $8.5 million in 1934 to expand the National Wildlife Refuge system (set up specifically for waterfowl initially). Salyer worked frantically, scrambling to make sure every dollar was spent, as it must be or be lost, by the March 31, 1935, deadline. He put the finishing touches on the program on the day the deadline came due, tirelessly and with great foresight creating the world's finest refuge system during a decade of great financial despair, worn out farm fields, and waterfowl crisis.

When he was done, bureaucrats unused to the action and fervor of a man with a passion for wildlife lay strewn in his wake. He had driven more than eight thousand miles, cornering the best waterfowl habitat he could find, inspecting every acre, all across America. By the time he had spent the $8.5 million, incorporating lands already in the public domain, Salyer had set aside fifty-five refuges for wildlife. Later, Salyer became Chief of the

Division of Migratory Waterfowl for the Bureau of Biological Survey, the predecessor of the U.S. Fish and Wildlife Service, and stayed on for more than twenty years.

I do not think Rascal's head came off my lap for the entire day, and when she slept on the seat next to me her feet twitched and she whimpered eagerly as she chased snow geese in her dreams. A great deal of comfort comes from traveling with a dog, at least a good dog like Rascal. I shudder to think how lonely my trip would have been without her. Always those brown eyes watched me. Always her tail wagged. As we drove she alternated putting her head on my thigh and on my right arm. Of course her value in a hunting situation was important, but even more important was the great pleasure I received in watching her work. Those of you who have working dogs know what I mean. The passion and drive they have is perhaps unmatched, whether it be a Labrador retrieving a duck or a husky pulling a sled. I doubt I would hunt birds if I did not have a good dog.

About midday we turned north at Dunseith. My eyes burned from the dust. Slowly we climbed in elevation until we popped into a hilly, forested country. So out of place was this oasis in the midst of the prairie that I slowed to nearly a stop, while angry truckers hauled down on their air horns to let this stupid tourist know they didn't appreciate his gawking. Aspens and oaks, a spruce or two, and shallow, woodland lakes greeted me—the Turtle Mountain Provincial Park.

In the midst of the mountains Turtle Mountain Park rolled down from the hilltop where the customs buildings straddled an imaginary line. Far ahead you could see the wheat fields spread out in a yellow haze, but nearby the trees were green and luxurious and the small potholes and lakes held water, some of the only standing water I had seen in a long distance. Ducks were beginning their afternoon travels, scurrying low over the cattails and hard-stem bullrushes. To see trees and water again was intoxicating. When a whitetail bounded across the highway, narrowly escaping a trundling semi, I decided that this place was too nice to pass up: I'd spend the night here. I set out to learn a bit about this country and find a quiet place to camp for the night.

The hills petered out quickly as I dropped to the plains beyond, leaving wistfully and for the moment the green and gold forest. Highway 10 arrowed its way onto the prairie and the waiting town beyond.

Boissevain, population 1,581, seemed to be just another town on the great mid-continental wheat desert. At least at first. I sensed a difference, though, after only a few minutes of wandering the streets, for there seemed to be an air of bustle, not the busy, harried bustle of big cities, the kind of bustle that wearies one just to watch it and stirs deep desires for escape, but the kind of bustle that belies constructive activity, people working and happy, moving about the street with definite missions but devoid of rush. I liked the feeling.

I pulled the truck over on the wide main street in front of a crisp, old brick building. A bank. Just what I was looking for. I needed to get more of that great, colorful Canadian money.

A woman smiled at me as I held the bank door open for her. I strolled into the dark interior, relief for my dust burned eyes. An attractive woman motioned me to the counter behind which she stood.

"Need to exchange some currency, eh?" she asked, smiling. I must have looked confused. I mean, did I have "Made in the U.S.A." plastered on my forehead? Lordy. Pointing out the window, obviously sensing my confusion, she simply smiled a wonderful smile and said, "Your truck." I looked. The giveaway Minnesota license plates.

I pulled out a stack of greenbacks, and she carefully counted them with the teller's swift thumb-stroke, replacing them with blue and white and red and green Canadian bills and a small pile of coins, a few of which were gold, octagonal, and about the size of a quarter.

"Loonies," she said, pointing to the coin emblazoned with the common loon, that noble bird of the north with the wonderfully haunting song. "The government's phasing out dollar bills and pushing these things on us. Smallest paper denomination now is the two-dollar bill. Nobody likes carrying around all these coins, but what are you gong to do, eh?"

I wanted to tell her, but didn't, about our Susan B. Anthony silver dollar and the two-dollar bill of the early 1980s. In typically American fashion, we had simply staged a quiet revolt. Supply and demand determined the extinction of both new denominations.

"Here for the hunting?" she inquired.

"Sort of. Could you tell me where I could go for some information?"

"Sure. That would be Burt Barwick's Sporting Goods. Did you come in from the south? You drove right past it as you came into town, eh?"

Thanking her, I stuffed the money into my wallet and stepped into the bright, warm day.

Burt Barwick's Sporting Goods is a squat little building on the south end of town, right on Highway 10. There is a small cafe right next door, appropriately called the Highway Cafe, with some sprawling shade trees and a sign that proclaimed "Good Food." Barwick's had a sign too: "Guided Goose Hunts." This must be the place.

The little shop was typical of the mom-and-pop sporting-goods stores and bait shops I had grown up habituating back home—disheveled and cluttered, but where, no doubt, you could find just about anything you might need. I liked it immediately.

"Burt?" I asked hopefully as a tall, older gentleman walked out from the back room.

"That's me. What can I do for you?" he replied, sizing me up.

The room smelled good, foul in a way, but good nonetheless. I looked past Burt, through the hall to the back room where geese were hanging. Down floated everywhere like a gentle snowfall in December, and a young man was the picture of industry as he rolled down and feathers from a plump snow goose. The odor, pungent but easily recognized by a water-fowler, was that of burning feathers as the remaining down was singed from the plucked carcass.

"Lady at the bank told me that you could be of help. I'm looking for a place to camp and maybe do a little hunting. It looks awfully dry, though. Are there any potholes around where a guy could throw out a few decoys and see some ducks?"

"You want to hire a guide?" he asked, studying me with the air of a judge (which he was, retired) evaluating a defendant's story. Pods of down clung to his nose and hair.

"No. Wish I could. Can't afford it, though. I'd just like to see some birds, mostly, although I wouldn't mind shooting a few."

"Geese or ducks?"

"Ducks. And water. I'd sure like to see someplace wet."

So, inevitably, the conversation turned to the drought, the ducks, and agriculture. The story here was almost identical to that in Saskatchewan.

"It's been awfully dry. You won't find any potholes around here. Even Whitewater Lake is dried up. When it dried up, it blew salt all over the area. Some of those people that lived to the south of the lake, why, their cattle quit eating their own pastures. The grass was just covered by that gray salt-dust, and the cattle got sick. You want to see something, you should drive over there. It used to be full of ducks and geese, thousands of them. Now its just a salt flat, eh?"

"I saw a lot of smoke west of here as I drove in. What's going on?"

"Oh, yeah? That's the worst part of this drought, eh? The farmers can really get in there and work over those sloughs. They burn them when they're dry, then plow 'em up."

I must have looked crestfallen. After seeing the lush Turtle Mountain Park, I had hoped things might be different here. The mountains were a park, though, so I knew I wouldn't be able to hunt there.

Barwick gave a slight sigh, probably just as despondent about the ongoing habitat loss as I was. Then he perked up.

"Well, you could hunt the mountains. Pretty good ruffed grouse hunting there, and some ducks. I think I have a park brochure around here somewhere. Lemme look."

"You mean I can hunt in a park?"

"Sure. Not everywhere, but in some parts. Stop at the park headquarters at Adam Lake. You can't miss it. It's almost back to the border," he said, handing me a brochure.

I thanked him, bought a large map of the region that showed land ownership, and, excited about the promise of it all, sped back south to Turtle Mountain Park. A stop at the ranger station provided me with information on where I could camp and hunt. Things were definitely looking up.

I'll tell you this. After nearly two weeks of being on the drought-ravaged prairie, I was ready to see water and forest. And I was feeling a good deal of sympathy for those who lived and worked on those prairies, despite my emotions regarding the ongoing destruction of wetlands. How those people must yearn for rain! To say that finding this oasis made me happy would be a vast understatement.

I pulled off the highway on a gravel side road that led downhill to Adam Lake. The campground was empty except for one occupied campsite. I backed the truck into a site near the lake, cranked up the camper, lit the gas refrigerator, and cleared the camper floor of decoys, coolers, and assorted other duffel. Behind me the sun was slanting low and orange on the rippling lake. Soft waves lapped on the beach.

Rascal and I strolled to the lake to watch the sunset and the comings and goings of the ducks. Sandpipers scurried on the beach. The wind was wet and fresh. Deer tracks were mirror-image commas in the sand. Leaves rustled.

Here the world was wet. For a while we could forget about the drought. There wasn't a desolate acre in sight. Rascal and I went to bed very happy.

A duck hunter's world is full of many things. Nocturnal walks where everything is squeezed into the narrow beam of a flashlight in the predawn hours. Decoys in a sack that bounces awkwardly against your back. A shotgun that hangs heavily, but with a solidly good feeling, at the end of your arm. Shotgun shells that rattle in your pockets. All of this after an early rising and dark drive down winding roads to a place that is still wild.

It is exactly because ducks like such wild places that makes duck hunting so addictive. These are not the same popcorn-fed birds you see in city parks, ducks and geese devoid of any wildness, trading the rigors of the marshlands, and therefore their very souls, for handouts. These are birds spawned in harshness and beauty, their very existence depending upon skills of survival, upon their adherence to a millenium's combined lessons passed down in their genes. Molecular wildness.

Ducks come from places far and savage where life functions as it should; the hunter comes from places where that life no longer exists, seeking it, needing it, to put balance back into life. And so paths cross, in moments unimaginable to those who are deskbound, in a place of random meeting.

Even in the darkness a duck hunter's world is rich. Smell the rank ooze of the marsh, bits of earth, sticks, leaves, bodies big and small, accumulated over the centuries. It is a sweet smell to the duck hunter, especially as he wades in rubber armor, his feet stirring the sediment and releasing trapped gases to bubble to the surface. In the darkness, a hunter also hears many things: the palaver of owls, the snort of a buck, unfathomable rustlings in the cattails, swift heart-stirring sweeping wings, the whistle of duck feathers in the night. A mallard hen, quacking contentedly in some marshy corner, talks to her flock, awakening it for the morning feeding flight. Retrievers whine solemnly in anticipation.

Our morning started with a quick breakfast and scalding coffee in the camper, the rapid breaking of camp, and the quiet ride through this wonderful forest, trying to remember which turns to take, and not wanting to arrive too late to see the sunrise and the ducks.

I pulled the truck to the side of the road, shut off the lights, and waited for my eyes to adjust to the dark before unloading, hitching up chest waders, and stuffing pockets with shells, sandwiches, duck calls, and all the other accoutrements of wildfowling. A half-mile hike through the woods brought us to one of the park's many scattered lakes. Brush scraped bare, cold hands and stung reddened cheeks as I lumbered through the undergrowth. Black Rascal flowed like a wraith through the woods.

The bottom of this little lake was such that if you stood still long enough you would inevitably join the myriad other creatures reposing in the mire. This morning the wading was aggravated even more by the half inch of solid skim ice that had formed during the night and reached out twenty or more yards from shore. Using one decoy as a club, and moving constantly to avoid getting stuck, I bashed my way through ice, making big holes for the decoys to sit, where they tinkled against the shards. By the time I was done with this task, despite the twenty-degree temperature, I was bathed in sweat. My chest waders, above the water, wore a sheen of ice from my splashing. Reaching up from below the curve of the world, the sun was already painting rose-colored clouds.

I tromped a little path into the cattails from the makeshift blind to the water. In this I sat Rascal, just to my right, so that she would be able to see any ducks that fell. I blew on my blue hands, trying to force them to work, but they were hopelessly frozen, so I thrust them down into my wader tops, sat on the folding stool, and waited for sunrise. On this day, October 11, the sun was due to rise at 7:45, which meant that legal shooting could begin at 7:15. I glanced at my watch. Fifteen minutes to go.

From the west they came hurriedly, whispering whistle of wings. Holding my breath to hear better, I made out the faint splashings as the morning's first ducks landed just beyond our decoys. Rascal was vibrating so hard her teeth rattled.

Finally, my hands thawed out enough that I could load the shotgun. I bent two clumps of cattails over in front of me and tied them together, forming a little rest to prop the gun against. I hung the duck and goose calls around my neck, and then, after standing up to make sure that I could see to shoot over the cattails, crimped over a few to clear the path. We were ready. The ducks, hearing my rustling, swam to the far shore, silhouettes on the silver lake.

The sky changed from pink to mauve. Songbirds whisked by. Muskrats munched and swam. High now, above the daybreak, I could make out flocks of ducks working into the northwest wind, specks on the horizon.

I looked at Rascal. Her cattail floor had sunk into the bog, and water was oozing up around her. God, that had to be cold on her ass. She gave no sign of noticing but I shivered involuntarily.

Both of us snapped suddenly toward a deep, thudding *crunch* working along the ridge behind us. Footsteps. Big ones. Rascal rumbled.

Then came a piercing whistle, a calliope of wildness. A bull elk, no more than forty yards away but still a shadow in the dawn, had tilted back his rack, pointed his hoary muzzle to the rising sun, and split the stillness with his bugling call. He said, in that single series of whistles, something about being king, challenges, mating, vitality, wildness, and even serenity. Then he stalked quietly away, leaving me feeling damn happy that I had chosen to be in this spot on this day.

Morning awoke with a gasp. A flock of gadwalls buzzed our decoys. I grabbed the duck call and shotgun simultaneously, playing one while readying the other. I could clearly see their flashing white speculums as they swung by again, this time coming into range.

"Stay," I reminded the dog as I crouched, ready.

I found a drake in the flock and sent a load of shot out toward him. Somewhere in space they met. With a few feathers floating on the wind, the gray duck tumbled to the lake, hitting the surface with a thump. Shit. The ice had re-formed.

Rascal was still just a pup and she had never retrieved through ice. If glaring eyes could melt ice, she would have no problem as she focused on the gadwall. I had no choice but to send her.

With the springboard leap of a Labrador, Rascal flew into the lake, whumping through the ice, shaking her ears free of the water of her splash. She stroked ten feet, front paws breaking ice, before she realized that something was wrong. She turned and looked at me.

"Good dog. Good girl. Dead bird," I said with encouragement. Waving an arm up and forward, I gave her a command.

"Back! Get back."

She turned. Ice cracked, crunched, flew, front paws whacking, back paws churning underwater. Her big, black tail ruddered behind her. The ice crumbled beneath her, the distance narrowed. Twenty yards, then ten. The gadwall was hers. She rotated in place and swam the ice-cube channel back to shore, heaved herself up onto the floating marsh mat, and spit the duck into my hand. She looked up at me.

"Sheesh, boss! What the heck was that?"

I smiled, called her a good dog, and rubbed her wet head. She stood streaming and steaming, happy. A test had been passed. If there had been any question in my mind before, it was now gone. She had heart. Plenty.

As pups, retrievers are curious and have attention spans and memories as short as their noses. Once they have been exposed to game, this all begins to change. Put a Labrador pup down on a lake shore, and it will watch the lake, chase butterflies, turn to sniff the forest behind, lick its paws, and generally goof off. Take that same pup, after two weeks of hunting, to that same shore and follow its gaze. It will intently scan the sky for ducks and geese. A dog is better than radar. And when the birds come, it will roll those wonderful chestnut eyes, following the flight with a minimum of motion, and wish, from its huge heart, that the fowl would come closer. I love retrievers.

More flocks came, and the scenario repeated itself; a plump wigeon joined the gadwall in a spot of honor in the duck blind. The sun was fully up, glaring on the water but not yet warm. Frost glistened on the cattails, and Rascal's muzzle was white. Steam rose from her in wisps. My breath was visible. The acrid odor of burned gunpowder spiced the air.

Nonhunters should understand that when waterfowlers are in the marsh it is not hour after hour of endless slaughter. Fooling ducks under the best conditions, without resorting to such illegal practices as baiting with grain or using live decoys, is difficult. Moments of activity are often punctuated by long periods of sitting, and for every flock shot at, a hunter probably sees many more that don't come within range. To pass time, duck hunters chat or study the surrounding environment. I have felt, on days when the ducks came fast and easy, cheated that I hadn't spent enough time in the marsh.

Today, during a lull, I picked up the handsome wigeon drake and laid him on my knees. His belly was white and elliptical, framed by his rich mahogany brown sides and chest. A fine specimen, this male was fast

America's Waterfowl

Although there are fifty-five species and subspecies of ducks, geese, and swans present in North America, most are seen infrequently. Limited numbers or special habitat requirements keep them out of sight.

The central part of the continent sees Canada geese, as well as white-fronted geese and lesser snow geese (and its color phase, the blue goose). Generally, geese have been doing well because they nest primarily in the Arctic, where man's influence has not been so severe. They have adapted well to feeding on agricultural waste grain in their wintering range. Additionally, sportsmen's groups and wildlife agencies in the States have re-established breeding populations of Canada geese in areas where they had been extirpated.

Canada geese number over 3,000,000 birds. White-fronted geese average close to 300,000 birds. In recent years, lesser snow geese have increased their numbers to about 2,000,000 birds.

gaining his nuptial plumage, dressing up for the courting rituals of the wintering grounds. His forehead was white (hence the nickname "baldpate"), and a narrow white band stretched back to the crown. His cheeks were salt-and-pepper, and the metallic green wedge from his eye to the back of his neck glinted. I spread the webbing of his blue-gray feet to feel its luxurious leather.

By comparison, the gadwall is a bland bird. Yet even this blandness can be admired for its ultimate camouflage effect. The white speculums were three feathers wide on the trailing edge of each wing and on this drake were bordered in black on two sides. Forward of this was a patch of chestnut brown. The remainder of the wing was primarily gray. This gadwall, too, had a white belly, rimmed in streaky gray.

I set the wigeon down on the grass and scanned the sky for more ducks. From the north a flock of six great, hooting, lumbering tundra swans swung over the lake. Their tremolo call reminds me somewhat of the

Although there are many more species, most of the ducks encountered in the midcontinent marshes will be the mallard, gadwall, wigeon, pintail, ringneck, lesser scaup, wood duck, redhead, and canvasback. Both green-winged and blue-winged teal are also common.

The most prevalent by far is the mallard. The drakes of this species are characterized by their brilliant green heads. An estimated breeding population of 5,500,000 mallards exists continentally, down substantially from even the 1970s, when nearly 9,000,000 were breeding.

Pintails, with their graceful long necks, dropped to 2,900,000 birds in 1986, a dramatic decline from 6,300,000 in the previous decade. Similarly, numbers of the early migrating blue-winged teal, with its wing coverts of robin's-egg blue, have plummeted from 5,300,000 down to 3,800,000.

In 1985, the continental breeding populations for other duck species were as follows: gadwall, 1,400,000; wigeon, 2,500,000; green-winged teal, 1,900,000; redhead, 706,000; canvasback, 411,000; and scaup, 6,200,000.

Thirty-four percent of all dabbling ducks, 24 percent of all diving ducks, and 31 percent of all geese winter in the Mississippi flyway.

hooting of an owl. How huge they are! Weighing up to eighteen pounds and measuring five feet in length, this species is smaller than the trumpeter swan, but their far greater numbers mean that these giant birds are seen by many more people during migration.

Speaking of migration, how do ducks know that the wind that howls from the north today is only a hint of winter's iciness? The lakes are freezing during the night and yet the ducks display no migration tendencies. They know that there will be a few more golden autumn days before the true onset of winter.

And how is it they return, year after year, to almost the same spot where they were born or where they nested before? What feats of navigation they accomplish, winging uncounted miles, searching the ground for landmarks, following great waterways, and using the stars to guide them!

This wigeon, a handsome gray drake, perchance had come from Canada's Northwest Territories, riding high over herds of caribou and the wolves that stalk them, past Great Slave Lake and the frothing rivers that feed it. His piping call certainly had been heard over the prairies. Had I not brought his beauty to hand, were he not destined for my dinner, he would have beat his way south and east, through Minnesota and Wisconsin, beyond the cornfields of Illinois, and over the blue hills of Kentucky, shortly to see the vast Atlantic. It is possible, as some wigeons do, that he would have streamed above the shining ocean, above the dancing porpoises, finally to spend his winter in Cuba or the Dominican Republic. What a journey!

My discomfort put an end to my musing. My feet were numb, and my knees ached. I stood up and looked over the cattails at the decoys. Despite the sun, the ice had re-formed into a jumbled mass that left the decoys lifeless. I'd have to fix that.

I finished breaking up the ice to set the decoys free to bob again in the north wind. Rascal stretched and raced around in the cattails, happy to be moving.

Just as I reached shore I heard a mallard hen quack. I stopped, hunched. Wings beat near. I could hear a flock come from the north, pass directly above my hat, swing back toward the lake, and then, with the throat-clearing rasp of set wings, drop to the water.

I peeked over my shoulder. The ducks, four of them, sat bolt upright, immediately sensing that something wasn't as it should be. Damn right it wasn't. I should have been in the blind watching smoke rise from my gun barrel. Rascal should have been out here in the lake, not me, fetching a fat greenhead. The ducks looked at me, a sidelong glance from the one hen meeting my eye, and launched themselves in a takeoff that would have made NASA proud.

That is duck hunting. And you thought it was easy.

With two ducks I had enough for a meal and so contemplated ending the hunt. One more duck, however, would ensure two days' dinners or some duck breasts left over for sandwiches. Besides, the morning was young and, although the best shooting was probably nearly over (a half hour before sunrise to a half hour after is the best), I had no desire to leave the marsh. Perhaps there would be more surprises like the elk.

I didn't have to wait long. A big, glossy, black beaver swam past our duck blind with no hint that we were there. He climbed out for a moment on an exposed mud bank near shore and sat in the morning sun, grooming his luxuriant fur. After his morning ablutions, the big rodent slipped quietly into the lake, his block-shaped head making a rippling wake as he swam toward the opposite shore. Then he disappeared into a channel in the reeds. Beavers construct such channels to give them access to the forest without having to leave the water. Though fairly mobile on land, a beaver is never comfortable without the safety of water nearby; the channels bring that security nearer as they work in the woods.

In this case the canal headed to the base of an aspen ridge where, if I knew my beavers, he was heading to do a little logging. A succulent aspen shoot is one of the beaver's favorite foods. This fellow was probably hauling huge quantities from the tops of felled trees to his lodge, submerging the shoots in the lake to keep them moist and to provide food for the winter.

The Turtle Mountain Park's undulating hills are lush with deciduous trees. I have seen aspen and ash, as well as birch and oak. The hills rise six hundred to seven hundred feet from the plains as a blue shadow, resembling the turtle for which it is named. Straddling the border between North Dakota and Manitoba, the hills were a landmark for travelers long before the white settlers ever came. These mountains were formed largely by vast amounts of glacial till plowed up at the end of the last ice age onto the more ancient bedrock. Glacial ice probably accounted for the many depressions that are now lakes and sloughs as large chunks broke off and melted, their vast weight denting the earth.

When the landscape became forested, it was no doubt the home to the gigantic mammoths and bison, which in turn invited nomadic human hunters to follow. Eventually, the present prairie that surrounds the forest took shape about ten thousand years ago, and the prairie fauna multiplied and adapted until bison, deer, elks, and antelope were found in staggering numbers.

In this area, the Plains Indians, primarily Sioux, hunted buffalo. The natives of the forest, Cree, Ojibway, and Assiniboines, also came to hunt this huge, shaggy giver of life. With these meetings came conflicts over hunting rights. Because the trees provided protection and fuel when hoary winter came, the hills became home for man and beast during the snowy months.

When the white man had finally eliminated the bison from the prairies, a way of life ended abruptly for the Indian peoples. Settlement followed, and the area around the Turtles is heavily farmed.

I saw farmers out pecking away at the ancient forest, even now clearing yet another acre or two, chopping right up to the park boundary. Today the forest exists only as a small reminder of the wildness that once was this part of Manitoba and North Dakota.

Rascal and I shared a peanut butter sandwich. I tore off small chunks and tossed them into the air, and like a magician she made them disappear. "Voila!" she smiled.

When the sky turned blue, the gray night clouds receding to the south, I stood to stretch my legs. Time to go. The morning had been rich. I had enough ducks for dinner and enough memories for years to come.

As I picked up the decoys, winding the cords about their keels and pinching the lead strap weights around their necks, a gaggle of snow geese wandered over our lake. Joyous in their calling, they were flashing beacons of life in the sky. Waterfowl are truly the voice of the prairie. Songbirds. I wondered, as had Aldo Leopold, what if there were no more goose music?

With the decoys bagged and on my back, I hung the ducks on a strap and slung them over my shoulder, grabbed my shotgun, and walked up the hill. Rascal raced.

I wandered down the trail, more slowly now in the daylight than I had in my hurry to beat the dawn. Rascal would grab a stick, puppy fashion, and romp, tossing it for herself and then making the retrieve. Then she stopped, as if realizing that she was no longer a pup; she had made good retrieves in tough ice. She ran back to me and heeled without a command, sniffing the ducks that hung down to my belt.

The sparse October woods were gray and brown, the few leaves gold. A cool breeze blew on my sweaty neck as I flumped along in chest waders. Rascal was ecstatic, sniffing and prancing.

Among all the elements that make up a duck hunter's world is one that is inevitable and especially sweet: a heavy, worry-free drowsiness. It stole over me slowly, creeping into my arms and legs first and then my mind. A nap was going to feel very good.

I felt myself to be a truly fortunate man.

———————————

Rascal's rumbling growl was so threatening it frightened even me and brought me quickly and fully awake. Footsteps crunched in the darkness outside the camper, first along one side of the truck, then the other, stopping twice. Rascal growled again.

Then there was deep, maniacal laughter, the kind that makes you think "Uh-oh!" when you hear it come from a character in a movie. But this was no movie, and the laughter came from more than one person. I was worried.

The footsteps faded away. I opened the curtain on the window nearest my bunk. Thirty yards away more than a dozen men stood around a huge bonfire. I could see a bottle being passed and two or three cradled guns. I was beyond worried. I was fast approaching frightened.

I looked at my watch. Midnight exactly. The witching hour. (Cut that out!) Here I was, camping by myself in a deserted campground on Max Lake with a dozen armed and probably drunk lunatics nearby—and someone had just been creeping around my truck. Now what?

I looked into the darkness again. Two men were turned my way, one gesturing toward my camp, a rifle limp in his arm. As they talked, someone else kicked the fire. It flared, lighting flushed faces. They were Indian. Again, the frightening laughter.

I didn't know whether or not they meant to do me harm, but I wasn't going to stick around to find out. I could guess what they had been up to. No doubt they had been out trying to kill a deer or moose. Treaty rights across North America allow the native people to kill animals for food. Since they are doing it primarily for subsistence, they are not overly concerned about the thrill of the hunt or a fair chase. The quickest, easiest way to kill a deer or similar game is to shine a spotlight into its eyes at night, and when the animal becomes transfixed, to shoot it.

I quietly slipped from the upper bunk and got dressed without turning on the lights, then loaded my shotgun. Rascal watched me. I moved her to the floor, told her to stay, put anything that might fall from the counters down with her, quietly lowered the camper roof, eased outside, tossed the decoys near the dog, latched two of the four roof clamps, threw the shotgun into the truck cab, and fired up the truck.

Somehow I had gotten this far without drawing attention to myself. When I turned on the headlights and pulled out, though, that all changed instantly: three men ran toward a pick-up and jumped in. Damn. I was being followed. My mouth was dry and my pulse raced. I could see their headlights in my rear-view mirror. I floored it.

Taking corners at high speed on a gravel road in a truck with a camper on it is nothing like the fun of cornering a sports car on a good road. It feels more like "Oh, shit. I think we're going to tip over if I don't go in the ditch first." I tried to anticipate the twists and turns of the road, hoping my memory didn't fail me. I wanted to get back to the highway, which, I hoped, meant safety. There would at least be other traffic there. Maybe a cop.

The heavy truck nearly became airborne on steep dips. I wondered about Rascal in the back. The lights were just behind me—and then they attempted to pass on the narrow road. I cut them off, swerving. Oh, lordy!

A yellow sign ahead marked an intersection. I turned left—hard!—not even looking for oncoming traffic. The rattle of gravel on the truck's underside gave way to the whining of tires on blacktop. I'd reached the highway and could see Boissevain a few miles ahead.

The truck behind me stopped, turned around, and returned the way we had come. I watched the one red taillight until it was out of sight. Only then did I pull over to see if I was still breathing.

The bastards were probably laughing their heads off.

I got out, unloaded the shotgun, went to the back of the truck, and opened the door. Rascal looked worried as she stood among pots and pans, duffel bags, dirty socks, decoys, and canned goods. I let her out, cased the gun, put her in the cab, and climbed in. In a minute, I had the truck pointed to the Adam Lake campground. It was near the highway and at least had some other folks camped there. I didn't think my new acquaintances would bother me there.

But I spent most of the rest of the night wondering about it.

After a night of fitful sleep, awakening at every sound, I finally got up and put on the coffee pot. It was four in the morning, and there would be no more sleep. I might as well go duck hunting. Rascal watched me from the upper bunk, the one we share that stretches above the truck cab. Whenever I slide from the sleeping bag, she takes the opportunity for an extra forty winks by burrowing into the still-warm bag, her black head on my pillow. Don't make a move for the door, though. She'll be up in an instant. No one goes hunting without Rascal.

I suppose some of you are wondering how, with numbers low, I can shoot ducks. I wrestled with that question before leaving Minnesota. A trip like this would be any waterfowler's dream, but it was my bad fortune to be doing it at a time when duck numbers were the second lowest in recorded history. Of course, there were more than sixty-four million ducks still in existence; obviously, they weren't in danger of extinction. Goose numbers were healthy—even expanding—so my moral trepidation did not extend to them.

I came to the following conclusion: I'd likely never get a chance to hunt these far-flung places again, and I would take the opportunity now, while I could, picking only drakes from species that were less threatened than others. Hunting mortality is generally compensatory; that is, when duck numbers are above a certain, hard-to-define, low threshold, hunting takes surplus birds from the percentage of the population that would have succumbed during the year anyway. I admit that this equation, which has worked well as long as there have been guidelines and laws to manage hunting, is now being questioned. Studies suggest that when duck populations fall below that threshold number, hunting mortality adds to natural mortality, thereby decreasing bird numbers. If the compensatory-mortality theory is correct, as most biologists believe, then environmental factors must be responsible for decreasing duck numbers. Biologists assured me that there was little harm in shooting a few ducks, especially if the hunter stuck to drakes. I decided I'd go one better. I'd also stop short of my limit. Moral wavering? Maybe. But there it is.

Rascal and I hunted the same little ice-rimmed, frosty lake with good success and returned in the afternoon to the campground at Adam Lake. During the day, we had wandered the park's back roads, watching the many ducks resting on quiet waters. At one point, a huge, nearly black bull moose stood on a reedy shore across the lake. We watched him until he lumbered into the forest. Still later, two moose, a small bull and a cow, appeared suddenly on the road and dared the truck to come nearer. I burst out laughing when Rascal sat rigid in the front seat, every hair at attention, growling at the moose. So brave—in the truck.

The burnished aspen forest was alive, and on the gravel road's grassy margins we spotted several ruffed grouse. One male, quite out of season, was doing a puffed nuptial display, rust fantail spread broadly.

Back at Adam Lake, we picked a different campsite just for the change. I set up camp while Rascal wandered. Then I set about the task of cleaning the ducks. I pulled out my knife, moved the campsite garbage can near the picnic table, and began to pluck.

"Had some luck today, I see," said a voice from behind me. Rascal and I both jumped.

I turned. Two middle-aged men stood amiably. My neighbors, I guessed, from the only other occupied campsite.

"Yes, guess I did. How about you? You hunting?"

Bob Jasinksi and Jon Gollmar were from New Lisbon, Wisconsin, and yes, they assured me, they had been hunting. This was their tenth autumn near Turtle Mountain. They were an interesting pair. Bob, balding and comical, was the perfect complement to his gruff, butch-haircut partner, Jon. Their verbal sparring, one could tell, was born of long friendship.

"Here, we'll give you a hand," Bob said. "Hey, Jon, why don't you run back and get those shears?"

In a flash, the three of us had the ducks cleaned. When we were done, Jon gave me the shears. I had admired how nicely they cut through the wing bones, and there was no refusing him.

Stammering, I said, "Thanks for the help and the shears. You didn't have to do that, you know."

"That's what being a sportsman is all about," answered Jon, "helping other people and sharing."

I liked that. I poured us each a tall scotch after putting the cleaned and wrapped ducks into the refrigerator.

"Whatcha doing for dinner?" Bob asked. "Care to join us for some barbecued duck breasts?" I said I sure as hell would. And I'd bring desert, some of my wife's cookies.

Another cold night was on the way. Somewhere nearby, geese were calling. The lake was a yellow pool of sunset. After feeding Rascal, I walked to their camp, with a gift of cookies and a bottle of scotch whiskey. There was a black Ford pick-up loaded with piles of duck-hunting gear. A canoe lay alongside. Attached to an ancient camper (circa 1964) was an amazing room made up of blue, green, and orange tarps strung on a framework of two-by-twos. Everything had been constructed in advance so that Bob and Jon just needed to assemble the precut pieces, like a child's building blocks. The room had a door to the outside and another to the camper, clear plastic windows, and lawn-chair furniture. Shelves holding food supplies were set up on the outside of the camper where it formed an inside wall of the room. An ingenious woodstove made of electrical transformer boxes glowed in one corner, its hot little stovepipe poking out through the one solid wall panel. Biscuits were being baked, as green beans simmered in cream-of-mushroom soup. Outside, a little Weber kettle waited with hot coals for the duck breasts.

As guests, Rascal and I were allowed to do nothing. Bob busied himself with the inside cooking; obviously, Jon was the master of the Weber. I poured the drinks.

We talked for a while as strangers talk, a little formal around the edges. Then the whiskey worked and the dog made friends. Soon I was comfortable with them. We spoke of ducks, the drought, hunting, and dogs. Equipment was compared. A shotgun with a custom stock was passed around for admiration. Jon occasionally brought in tidbits of grilled duck breasts to whet our appetites.

I remember Jon standing in the corner of the room, his face glowing and arms waving with excitement as he described the decoying of this morning's ducks. Duck hunters are like that. Ducks trigger passions that the serious hunter reveals unabashedly, in a way he never would if he spoke on any other subject.

Hunger overtook our conversation, and for a short while there was only the energetic eating of those whose appetites had been fanned by fresh air. The duck breasts were perfect: the pink centers were warm and the outsides were glazed with tangy sauce. Green beans and biscuits filled in the corners of our hunger. There was no room for the cookies.

After dinner, we talked more of hunting, dogs, guns, and knives. Bob diligently worked on the blade of my duck-cleaning knife, honing it to a razor edge. When he was done, he nonchalantly put it in his own sheath, one he had made himself, and handed it back to me. "I kind of like your sheath," he lied. We discussed politics and religion. We laughed at silly jokes. Jon got gruffer and more humorous, his language becoming "colorful." Bob, at my request (he's in the appliance business), tried to explain to me how my camper refrigerator could make cold from the blue propane flame. Even after his explanation, I relegated the flame-induced ice to the "miracle" category I save for technology I'll never comprehend. Occasionally, we went outside to see the stars and water the turf in the black Manitoba night. Rascal stretched out near the glowing stove.

When I had drunk enough (too much?), I got up to leave, reluctant but with still enough good sense to get myself to bed at a reasonable hour. I left the cookies.

"Would you like to hunt with us tomorrow?" Bob asked.

"I'd love to, but I'm heading north in the morning."

"Too bad. Maybe some other time. You'll probably find us here next year, same time."

"Hey, don't work too hard," Jon said, alluding to my task and every duck hunter's dream.

"Yeah, send us a postcard," added Bob. I told them I would.

We shook hands. I walked back in the dark, weaving a little, already feeling very lonely.

Whitewater Lake was indeed dry, just as Burt Barwick had said. Rascal and I drove as near to its shore as we could, taking a gravel road from Highway 3, north and a little west of Turtle Mountain. Whitewater Lake resembled a salt flat, something you might expect to see in the desert Southwest. Wisps of wind made little white tornados on the parched lake bed. It was staggering to think that this is one of the greatest waterfowl staging areas in Manitoba; all it gathered now was dust.

We had left the campground early in the morning, then stopped in Boissevain, where I showered at the municipal campground before going to the Highway Café for a breakfast that was both good and big. As in all small towns, the café was a focal point for locals. Businessmen and farmers sat together at one large, central table. Everyone pours his own coffee. A pair of Mounties strode in, and I took the opportunity to tell them of my midnight experience a few days before. It seemed to come as a surprise to them.

The café had strangely angled walls and ceilings. Poor-quality wildlife art and mounts decorated the walls. The people were extremely friendly, and for the first time since I'd been on the prairies, the coffee was very tasty, probably owing to the good water I'd noticed in the area. No doubt the nearby hills had some effect on the water table.

Weighed down with eggs, ham, potatoes, and toast, I paid my bill and headed toward Whitewater. I was on my way to see what I could find of the famous Manitoba wetlands.

Endless tan fields of wheat stubble whizzed by the truck. At Deloraine, we turned north and watched for signs of water. Not a pothole—or a duck—in sight.

Late in the morning, we turned west from Highway 21 to Oak Lake. This lake, too, is an important staging area for waterfowl. Fortunately, it held water, although judging by the receded shore the water level was low. A number of summer cottages were clumped on the east shore. A few duck boats were pulled up on the gray mud in front of the homes of those who were fortunate enough to have lakeshore property. We followed the sandy road that headed south along the lakeshore past the last of the cottages. A flock of Hungarian partridge, an introduced species, flushed from the tall grass alongside the truck and flew, unconcerned, within feet of the windshield for twenty or thirty yards, gray-and-rust-feathered rockets, matching our speed. Rascal came unglued. The birds tipped off to one side and vanished into a stand of tall, tan phragmites.

Occasionally, the road was blocked by small sand dunes. When one especially large dune blocked the road I stopped the truck. Even with four-wheel drive, I didn't want to risk getting stuck in a place like this. We'd walk from here.

On a gray sky with a stiff northwest wind came a flock of Canada geese. Dipping and twisting, blown up, blown down, calling all the while, they fought the wind. Passing just above us as we hid in a stand of wind-twisted willows, they landed just offshore. Rascal was ready to pounce. I made her sit, then joined her. For a long time we watched the geese bob in the waves. A few came to shore to primp. Yellowleg sandpipers played tag with the surf. Small flocks of ducks whisked rapidly over the waves. Too far out for positive identification, I knew at least that they were diving ducks by their quick wingbeats. There was no sign of human activity, and I liked it that way.

The vibrancy of this land when it is coupled with the sustaining waters continues to amaze me. One could drive one hundred miles and see little sign of life and then, suddenly encountering water, find a landscape flushed with vitality. Small mammals scurry across roads. Red-tailed hawks soar. Ducks, geese, swan, cranes, sandpipers, terns fly and feed. White-tailed deer bound into the tall rushes, flags flying and marking their path.

Finally cold, we returned to the truck and continued north, crossing the Trans-Canada Highway near Griswold, and then shortly passed over the great prairie river the Assiniboine, a highway of another sort. This river served as a route for the voyageurs, those intrepid canoemen of the 1700s. Sieur de la Verendrye paddled down this river, portaging near the present town of Portage la Prairie. From here he led his 1738 expedition to the unexplored northwest, opening the western territories of Canada to the lucrative fur trade of the era, a vein through which a nation's wealth could flow to Montreal. In the valley we passed an Indian reservation, houses all alike, spreading along the rolling hills and hemmed in by pastures and more wheat fields.

North of the valley the land grew flat again, and small farms dotted the countryside. I had yet to see a pothole, a fact that was beginning to worry me. Like all anxious waterfowlers from the south, I had for years waited to hear the annual reports of duck-nesting success, the counts of spring ponds, and all the other factors that may lead to a growth in duck populations.

They would portend what the coming hunting season might be like. And like all those other waterfowlers, I pictured in my provincial mind the rolling prairies to be both endless and undeveloped, almost limitless expanses of grass flecked with water. To think that I had driven this great distance without seeing a water-filled pothole was staggering to me.

For the past half hour, I had seen distant pillars of smoke towering above the flat landscape. Curious, I crossed the tracks of the Canadian National Railway, and somewhere south of Hamiota I turned onto a gravel road that would put me near one of the burns. A mile from the highway, I pulled to the shoulder of the gravel road and stepped outside. Just beyond the ditch, a wall of yellow flames was rapidly devouring a prairie pothole. I was taking pictures of the fire when a pick-up truck rattled to a stop beside me.

"What do you think you're doing?" gruffed a grizzled man in a seed-company hat.

"Shooting photos of this pothole on fire. Am I on your property?"

"Not unless you step off the road. What's the big deal with the fire?" he challenged, arms crossed on the window ledge.

I didn't know quite how to explain what I was doing—or maybe I just didn't want to. "Oh, I'm interested in ducks. You sure don't leave much room for them," I said, pointing to the burning wetland.

He glanced at my Minnesota license plates, looked me squarely in the eye, and, spitting a brown stream of tobacco juice in the dirt near my feet, said, "Don't farm ducks. Farm wheat." With that he threw the still-running truck into gear and sped away.

There, in a nutshell, is a large part of the problem. Two things really worried me: this guy could breed, and he could vote.

I had noted that for every farm that was restoring habitat, there were ten neglecting or destroying it. One step forward and two back. This farmer, burning the pothole, obviously was sensitive to the fact that some thought it wrong. But this was his land, and, by God, he was going to have his way with it.

The first rule of land stewardship is to not reduce the land's long-term productivity. The second is to not knowingly extirpate the creatures that depend upon the land. This man was following neither of these rules. Wind was blowing his topsoil away, and with a simple match he had set aflame the last of the wildlife habitat on his property. When the ashes cooled he'd get his heavy machinery in there and scrape, level, and plow the pothole. And what would he get for his labors? A bushel of wheat, maybe two. What drives such people?

Evolution determined the wealth of this land, built it so that this man's crops could find nutrients. Potholes kept the water table primed. Ducks, geese, plovers, horned larks, mink, deer, owls, muskrats, and bobolinks

Politics and Ducks

Although farmers in both Canada and the United States have been the immediate cause of habitat destruction, government policy sponsored by the general public is largely to blame. For decades, the U.S. Department of Agriculture has instituted policies and subsidies that encourage fencerow to fencerow farming at great financial expense to the public and to the detriment of highly erodable soils and marshes. These subsidy programs continue in the United States although recently more conservation practices have been incorporated into farm policy.

In Canada, the Federal Wheat Board sets a quota for each farmer, based on acres in production, as to how much grain he can sell to the government. By basing sales on acres plowed, the government encourages farmers to put more land into production. For example, if a farmer can grow more wheat on his prime land than the quota will permit him to sell, he simply needs to put more land into production, even if the yields are poor, to raise his quota.

Tax laws often encourage habitat destruction. "Improvements" on land for agricultural purposes can be used as tax deductions in Canada. Forested land is assessed at nearly the same value as cropland, but yields the farmer no profit. He is therefore encouraged by tax policy to clear and plow that habitat since his tax levy is high.

Many farmers are willing and happy to return land to wildlife habitat when new policies help them defray the cost. Both the Quill Lakes Project and the Chase Lake Project are encouraging good land stewardship through the use of cash incentives.

played their roles in the food chain, depending upon and feeding other creatures above and below them on the ladder. Better than half of all prairie birds are ground nesters, needing undisturbed protective cover. What fool would believe that he could eliminate that web of life and expect the land to still nurture him?

Beyond the practical considerations, who is this person to deprive wild creatures of life and rob the rest of us of the beauty, the songs, and the spiritual nurturing that wildlife gives? Does this man not have a soul? Thief!

For the past thirty years this man, and others like him, have treated the environment as an enemy and have spent huge sums to fight it, often with tax dollars. These are not the family farms you picture with green rolling hills, shade trees, a multitude of crops, and chickens and cows strolling in the lushness. They disappeared with the advent of monoculture farming just a few decades ago. These are farms where every inch of land is either road or wheat field. Even the ditches are plowed. Contemporary farming, whether done by small farmers or corporate agriculture, is characterized by the consumption of large amounts of fossil fuel and huge quantities of synthetic fertilizers, pesticides, and herbicides that contaminate well water, rivers, and lakes. Today's farmers practice continuous monoculture farming, draining the soil and depleting the space allowed for woodlots, hedgerows, and other windbreaks that would help to prevent soil erosion.

We all, every day, make ethical choices in our lives. The good citizen weighs the needs of the community along with his own when making such choices, for our civilization depends on such order. Sometimes the correct choice costs us something in dollars spent (or not earned) or in inconvenience. But in the long run we benefit. We are stronger and so is the community.

Why, then, does this philosophy not extend to the use of land? It too is a community—a biotic community—and one in which we are only a part. Is it not proper to expect a farmer, who claims to be a steward of the land and whose entire wealth comes from the resilience and health of that land, to make responsible choices? Can he not consider something besides wheat, such as the needs of creatures that cannot move elsewhere? He should, at the very least, consider that his own long-term prosperity depends upon the proper stewardship of the land.

We have contributed to our own demise and that of wildlife through our encouragement of the overproduction of crops by supporting commodity prices, by funding drainage, and by demanding cheap food. The

United States and Canada raise far more grain than they need. What isn't consumed by the residents of those countries is either fed to cattle or exported. In the United States, we have steadily been mining our soil to produce a product that we can sell abroad. This practice is encouraged by our government as a means of offsetting our huge trade imbalance. Our gluttonous taste for foreign goods is, in large part, one reason why we so abuse our natural resources. We have been trading topsoil for Toyotas and mallards for video cameras.

Will we change? Nearly half a century ago Aldo Leopold wrote this: "An ethical obligation [to the land] on the part of the private owner is the only visible remedy." Have we learned anything since then besides how to foul the land more quickly and how to hurry extinction? The solution is as clear now as it was then, and it is equally unpopular. Such brilliantly simple solutions are usually doomed to failure.

I sped north, putting distance between me and that farmer. Potholes became more numerous and many had water in them, a fact that likely saved them from being burned. A few even held ducks.

I stopped at the town of Shoal Lake for fuel. A young man came out to fill my tank. Two teenage girls sat outside the station drinking Cokes.

"Going hunting?" he asked, leaning on the truck while the fuel flowed.

"Maybe," I answered. "Have you seen any ducks around?"

"Sure there ain't much for ducks around here anymore. Not like it used to be." (This from someone who was barely twenty.) "Lots of geese, though. My pa and I shot our limit of snows this morning, eh? Right outside town. Your dog—she hunt?"

"Oh yes, she's a good one. Anyplace around here to camp?"

The campground that the boy had recommended was right in town. The list of rules at the entrance was two feet deep and three feet wide. "NO DOGS ALLOWED." I turned the truck around.

Through my binoculars I could see that Shoal Lake was about four miles long and only a few hundred yards wide in places. Hard-stemmed bullrushes rimmed the lake. Waves made white foam on the gravel beach, hinting at the water's salinity. Big flocks of starkly white snow geese loafed along the west shore. A few Canadas were mixed in. I could see only a handful of ducks.

Geese are a lesson. By and large nesting north of man's intervention and capable of subsisting on waste grain and the small bodies of water left in the wintering grounds, geese have proven more adaptable than ducks.

The giant Canada goose, the race of the species that was reintroduced by game departments and sportsmen's clubs, now nests in the middle and northern latitudes of the midwestern states and prairie provinces of Canada. Unlike ducks, whose numbers are further threatened by rapidly expanding populations of predators caused by the ecological imbalance of the land, geese can drive off a fox or skunk and so have better nesting success. It is also interesting to note that in spite of increased hunting pressure on geese, their numbers have grown. I almost despised them their success.

North again, then east. On Sandy Lake, north of the highway, I again saw great flocks of snow geese. The country turned to rolling hills, aspen groves, and smaller wheat fields—there were even some dairy cows. Most of the potholes were low or dry, but more-permanent lakes were sprinkled across the amber land. This is lovely country. To the north lay the blue hills of Riding Mountain National Park.

It was getting late. Rascal was antsy, and I was still annoyed with the tobacco-spitting bog burner. I wandered some back roads in search of seclusion, and finally, in the forest and hills south of the park, made camp beneath the trembling aspen, hidden from everything except my thoughts.

I like living in my little camper. There is a three-burner stove near the door. Beneath it are some cabinets and drawers and a propane furnace. I have a small sink with a hand pump. There is (believe it!) duck motif wallpaper on the wall. My refrigerator makes ice cubes for my scotch and sodas. Across from the stove and sink is the dining area: a small table on stilts that folds down to turn the seats into a bunk. Above the cab, at the back of the camper, is the main bunk. Beneath that is more storage. Two small closets are neatly stashed, one on each end of the "hallway."

When I make camp I first have to haul out the clutter: decoys, a cooler, waders, camera gear, shotguns, and a dog crate. Then I can unlatch and crank up the camper roof. The area between the hard roof and the hard sides is canvas with screen and vinyl windows. The camper has electric lights.

I eat primarily out of cans when I don't have a duck or grouse to cook. While the food is simmering, I pour myself a big drink and write or read. I have a portable radio and if I can find a classical or jazz station to listen to, I leave it on. Rascal doesn't talk much and is generally the better company for it. When I talk to her, she cants her head, her ears perked and her eyes bright.

By the time dinner is done and the dishes are washed (a little difficult to do in the shoebox sink), it is usually late. When the nights are cool, the furnace kicks in with a jetlike roar, then quiets down to the hum of the electric blower.

Before bed, Rascal and I take a walk. The stars are bright on clear nights. The colder it gets, the clearer they are. Sometimes we hear coyotes yipping across a field. Rascal reads each night to me through her sniffing and snorting, and I thank her for the interpretation.

When I have seen a billion stars and when Rascal has read a thousand scents, we climb back into the camper. I wash up, Rascal has a long drink of water, and we climb onto the top bunk together. The dog makes three tight circles, clockwise, and plops down next to me. She seems to take great delight in her bedtime fanfare. When I turn out the lights, there is a race to see who starts snoring first. We both dream about ducks. Do I run and twitch in my sleep, too?

Lynch Point, Lake Manitoba. Rascal runs in the gray surf, crashing through three-foot waves. There is nothing to fetch, nothing but rolling water, frothed with white and empty to the dim horizon. She is running and swimming, bobbing in the waves with the joy of a Labrador too long pent up. Loping out of the surf, she stops to lick my hand. There is joy in her eyes.

Along the beach scamper yellowleg sandpipers. Only moments before, a wedge of tundra swans rowed diligently into the north wind, their long necks undulating. Sheets of gray clouds, spread thin by the brisk wind, stipple the sky to the reach of every horizon.

We stroll along the beach. Hard-stemmed bullrushes are whipping in the waves far out into the lake. Flag-topped, yellowed phragmites stand back for protection. Terns, in a hurry, swoop on the wind like flights of sparrows. The world is gray and wild. The wind, cold and moist, blows in my face. My eyes water. I stoop to taste the lake. I relish salt, sloughs, marshes, meadows, fish, and birds.

One of the three large lakes (the other two are Lake Winnipeg and Lake Winnipegosis) of central Manitoba, Lake Manitoba is, as are the others, a remnant of the giant inland sea that formed behind the receding, melting glaciers of the last ice age. This particular remnant of glacial Lake Agassiz is twisting and narrow, nearly 115 miles long. At its widest, Lake

Manitoba spans 30 miles, the distance across which I was currently scanning. Shallow and sandy, the lake's many marshes contain a wealth of wildlife. To the north of Lake Manitoba are the myriad lakes of the boreal forest; to the south, the prairie—a division of worlds, habitats, and ways of life.

We had left our aspen hideaway very early this morning and drove to the hilltop village of Onanole and stopped for breakfast at the Old Hotel Café. Someone must have told them I was coming. As had been usual in Canada, the egg yolks were pale yellow and the ham, always of questionable quality, must have come from the first pig ever to have won the Kentucky Derby. I wrapped the meat in my napkin for Rascal.

Another man who was also sitting alone had been bow hunting for deer. It was inevitable that two hunters chat, especially so in friendly Manitoba. When I asked about his luck, he replied, "Didn't even see a deer. Damn near froze my ass off, though."

He glanced out the window at my truck.

"Thought you were a southerner, eh? You have an accent."

I choked on my coffee. Me, a southerner! From Minnesota!

I've learned much about our neighbors to the north. They are more like Americans than they like to admit. They drive more American cars than do Americans. They are competitive. If you are on the prairies, everyone assumes you too are a farmer. The most frequently asked question of me: "What crops do you raise?" They assume that Americans are richer than they are and always ask about prices in the States. Where I've been, they smoke more than we do. They resent the metric system. All in all, they like Americans. And I like Canadians.

Back on the road, Rascal dined on the "ham" while I drove south toward Erickson through hilly country with only small farms. I was pleased to see some spruce and tamarack among the oak and aspen, reminding me of home. To the south, where the land flattened a bit, lay the famous Minnedosa pothole region, an area that for centuries has been an incredibly productive breeding area for waterfowl for untold centuries. Less numerous than they once were, these wetlands still exist in great numbers, although the quality of nearby nesting habitat has been severely degraded. These two important pothole regions lie on the southern edge of what is known as the parklands. Unlike their prairie counterparts, parkland potholes are often located on aspen uplands. Because it is very likely that the parkland potholes were once prairie potholes that were gradually surrounded by trees as the forest marched southward, the two types have very nearly the same fertility and, therefore, productivity. The parkland forests have better withstood the onslaught of drainage, for only recently has any serious attempt been made to convert the aspen uplands to agriculture. In drought years, these potholes become even more important as waterfowl habitat. Because of their northerly location and the fact that the forests act as fences to trap and retain the snow, which melts to refill the marshes each spring, they are less prone to going dry.

It wasn't difficult, unfortunately, to find where man had begun to peck away at the forests surrounding even these hidden wetlands. A drive through the countryside revealed industrious destruction at nearly every turn in the road.

H. Albert Hochbaum, the great waterfowl researcher of the Manitoba prairies, laid the foundation for all researchers following him. In the prologue to his classic book *The Canvasback on a Prairie Marsh*, he wrote this: "Man's attitudes towards a marsh and a mountain are much the same; both must be conquered. The mountain is conquered so that it may be used, the marsh that man may be rid of it."

This was a strange echo of Aldo Leopold's words: "Progress cannot abide that farmland and marshland, wild and tame, exist in mutual toleration and harmony."

Leopold wrote his words in 1941, Hochbaum wrote his in 1944. Half a century hasn't served to make us wiser, only to make us more efficient at destruction.

We headed east, down Mountain Road and eventually across Provincial Road 265 through the town of Plumas. As we neared Lake Manitoba, its influence could be felt. The land was flatter and brushier, and the farms were less productive. In some places you could see that nature had won the battle with agriculture. Small, abandoned clearings grew up in a tumble of young aspens and brush as farms failed.

Halfway between Plumas and Langruth the road bisected Big Grass Marsh, another of Manitoba's famous wetlands. At a small pool of water alongside the road, I stopped the truck. Four gadwalls and a blue goose flushed from the ditch.

Standing on the step bumper of the truck, I scanned the marsh for ducks and geese. Little water was evident, either because Big Grass, too, was suffering from the drought or because the flat landscape with tall reeds and rushes made viewing difficult.

Aside from the lack of water, the drought had caused one other serious problem for Big Grass, a severe outbreak of avian botulism. Toxic bacteria quickly reproduce in warm, damp areas, such as an almost-dry marsh. The high death rate caused by this outbreak was at least partially responsible for the lack of waterfowl in the area.

Big Grass *felt* empty, just a sea of waving grass stems whipping in rattling unison in the wind, although birds probably hunkered in its interior. And the sky, which should have been stitched with strings of fowl, was instead a gray void. The spectacle of migration that has inspired writers and artists, stirred the imaginations of children, and brightened the lives of men and women toiling on chill autumn days was hardly to be seen. The migration trickled instead of poured, had to be sought when it should have demanded awe.

The marshland chorus is hushed. Ageless traditions teeter. I don't think I have ever felt more cheated in my life: cheated because I was born a century late, cheated because the spectacle that so many men before me had depicted as darkening the sky was now a memory, and cheated because it was not an act of God or quirk of nature but the diligence of man that had so impoverished this marsh.

That had been our morning. Our afternoon was wetter, wilder. A giant had been strolling atop the gray clouds above Lake Manitoba. I could see from Lynch Point where his trail had gone, to and fro, punching rounded footprints to bulge beneath the plain of gray. Where the clouds had torn loose, slivers of blue beamed through; the rest of the outlines were seamed in white. The flat clouds blew south before these bulging new ones advancing from the north.

As we walked the beach, a flock of diving ducks, rapid wings nearly brushing the water, scurried by, heading south. Rascal pivoted, tracking their flight.

A fine mist blew in from the lake, clinging damply to my skin and coating my eyeglasses. A cold, light rain followed. Maybe the rains of autumn would bring some relief to the prairie. Maybe the snows that followed would endow the land with a wealth of water.

I was anxious to head south. The cold wind stirring from the north, the sight of ducks winging south, and the November look to this October sky stirred in me a warm feeling in the face of cold. I had come to sense the migration, to see what the ducks saw, to go where they went. This was it. The migration was moving. I knew it as certainly as if I had been a part of it.

Rascal and I walked back to the truck, ready to find a place to camp for the night. I wanted to be near the birds so that in their departure they might call to me. I did not want to be left behind.

There was a little of Manitoba I still wanted to see, two days' worth, maybe three. Then, south.

I hoped the ducks would wait.

It came upon me like a fit. Now, without delay, no matter that darkness was closing its shady grip upon the land—I had to go south.

I'd like to believe that deep in my ancestral memory there was something that, sensing the winter, exhorted movement. And I didn't want to admit what I knew was the true motivation: that I had grown utterly depressed. What I had seen and heard had so rattled my ingenuous inclination to put my faith in the resilience of nature that I wanted to flee.

The past two days had been spent talking to waterfowl biologists and walking in the famous Delta Marsh. I did no hunting. I watched and listened and learned.

There are so many complicating factors to waterfowl management. Land use resulting in loss of habitat is paramount, but other factors are also critical. Change one and the others are modified, becoming more important.

For instance, what role does subsistence hunting by Indians play when it is done in spring on mostly paired, successfully breeding birds? How about crippling losses, those uncounted birds that are not figured into hunting season lengths, limits, and bird population numbers? What is the effect of hunting ducks on the breeding marshes? Are the successful breeders, those homing birds, being killed before they ever get a chance to disperse? What role does poaching play, especially in the wintering areas of the Deep South, where the illegal kill can exceed the legal harvest?

One researcher with fifty years' experience held no hope for the duck recovery. He was convinced that global warming had so modified prairie weather that droughts would continue to be a way of life. He also was adamant about closing the hunting season. Not an opponent to hunting (he was going grouse hunting as we talked), he insisted that hunting should

Avian Botulism

Avian botulism is a devastating disease that affects both waterfowl and shorebirds. It develops from toxic bacteria that are activated by hot, dry weather and low water conditions and is exacerbated by the crowding of the birds due to drought-induced habitat loss.

Paralysis affecting the duck's legs and internal organs is followed by a loss of strength in the bird's neck. Unable to hold its head up, the duck eventually drowns. The festering carcasses spread the disease.

Birds can be treated for botulism by antitoxin injections during the early stages of the disease. However, treatment is virtually impossible because of the rapid spread of botulism, the vast numbers of birds involved, and the large, difficult-to-penetrate habitats. Efforts to control the disease generally focus on collecting dead or dying birds and burning or burying them en masse. Cool, wet weather helps to slow the spread of avian botulism.

Manitoba's Whitewater Lake was the scene of an outbreak that killed fifty thousand waterfowl in the early 1960s. In 1980, Oak Lake's contamination resulted in the death of twelve thousand waterfowl. Avian botulism has struck in many places where waterfowl gather, including Minnesota and North and South Dakota.

The intervals between outbreaks are growing shorter as waterfowl are forced onto fewer and fewer pieces of habitat. And as duck numbers decrease, the losses are more significant.

have been stopped for the past three years, that the only way ducks will rebound is to cease hunting them for an undetermined period of time.

Finally, one researcher brought out the perplexing problem of predation. Expanding populations of skunks, foxes, raccoons, and crows destroy unprecedented numbers of duck nests.

Delta Marsh was beautiful with deep stands of wild hay and ducks trading from lake to marsh, from marsh to field, beneath the smoky October sky. Yet I left there feeling uneasy because, after all, this famous marshland was so small, so vulnerable to the farms to the south and the summer cottages that had sprung up around its edge. In the years since

Hochbaum had worked out of the Delta Research Station, duck populations here have declined dramatically. Manipulation by man, including some by waterfowl researchers, changed the way water from Lake Manitoba entered and left the marsh, leaving it less productive. Delta, the largest and at one time most productive of all marshes of the Lake Manitoba basin, had not withstood the past fifty years untouched. These marshes are truly fragile; even the most famous and productive are rimmed by development.

As I left the area it occurred to me that the urgency I felt might be the ducks' urgency, the call of migration. And maybe the cornered feeling that had claimed me, the sense that the world had suddenly grown very small and that there were few places left wild and in balance, was also what ducks felt. If it was, I empathized with them more than ever.

I flipped the cab light on and spread the Manitoba road map across the steering wheel. A tail wind buffeted the truck. South. I wanted to get south. But how far tonight?

A patch of yellow and blue at the bottom of the map grabbed my attention. Turtle Mountain. I felt a warm feeling. Yes, I'd camp tonight at Turtle Mountain.

Rascal laid her head on my lap as I turned out the light. The north wind pushed us south.

I had hoped that Bob and Jon were still at Adam Lake, but their campsite was empty—and so was I. Strangely empty. Maybe it was the loneliness of the open road. In the darkness the north wind made whirlpools of fallen leaves, pivoting yellow in my headlights.

We made camp near the lake. The night was frigid enough to make ice again. Waves hissed along the sand beach. I wondered if the ducks had stayed or if they, too, had moved on.

You have to really *want* to hunt ducks to get up at zero-dark-thirty in the morning after pushing until nearly midnight the evening before. I really wanted to hunt ducks.

Somehow it seemed that the only way to shake my mind clear of the dismal discussions with biologists, the encounter with the idiot with the matches, and the mile after mile of blowing topsoil and dry potholes was to get into the duck blind. I needed to see that nature can prevail, that ducks do indeed still make more ducks, and that the timeless rhythms yet pulse. Some of my friends have given up duck hunting because they feel that the best way they can help to solve the current duck problem is to stop shooting the birds. There is a great deal of sense to that. It is just that I can't do it.

One of my neighbors, a nice lady, once told me that the only reason duck hunters like me were active in saving wetlands is so that we could have more ducks to kill. There is some truth to that. It also falls far short of the whole truth. I think that the best thing I can do for the ducks is to go to the marsh, smell the mire, feel the briskness of an October dawn, let my soul recharge, and sit and think. Think about what a sad place the world will be when we have eliminated the last pothole and plowed the last mallard nest into the dust. To know, to *really* know the marsh, you must spend time there: you must be there at sunrise when the ducks fly, see the sandpipers strut, listen to the muskrats munch. And only when you know the marsh will you know what it is we may lose. Many kinds of people profess a concern for wildlife, but I have never met anyone but another hunter in a marsh.

Rascal and I returned to a Turtle Mountain marsh at dawn. The ice was so thick that a decoy would not serve as a maul and so I hunted up a fallen aspen, thick as my calf and ten feet long, and bludgeoned the ice from the shore to open water. I set six decoys bobbing in the hole.

When the morning yawned pink and purple, when the black clouds were lit to gray, when the dawn had breathed a wind, the gaudy mallards came. I heard a hen squawking from beyond the trees and watched as a dozen black forms streamed over the treetops, contouring the hill. I did not call. I said nothing to Rascal. If the ducks were going to come, I would let them, but I would do nothing other than hope that they saw the decoys.

Oh, God, did they see the decoys! The angry old biddy of a hen chewed out my fake birds for not answering her and led her flock in a wide arc, disappearing from sight behind the trees to our rear, only to drop from the sky coming in from our right.

I dared to peek from beneath my hat brim. There were drakes. I found a rust-chested, silver-sided bird in front of my gun, rose and shot without being conscious of doing so. Three pounds of green-headed prairie magic tumbled to the water.

Rascal looked at me. I was very pleased she had stayed put. I leaned over her, used my hand on edge as a pointer down her snout, and sent her to retrieve. She walked on water for the first ten feet.

The big duck was mortally wounded but not dead. He dived as the dog neared, and she turned, treaded water, and waited. The mallard came up for air. The dog spun to the sound. The duck dived. The dog plowed water, her breathing a wheezing bellows. Up came the duck again. Rascal surged. Each dive was shorter, and with each surge the dog was nearer. They met, Rascal going under with the duck's last dive. When she surfaced, she was breathing through mallard feathers.

When Rascal handed me the duck, I gave her great praise. I hefted the bird, my hand around its chest. I could feel its heart beating. Its wild eyes met mine. I turned my face. The duck shuddered, died. I faced it as its eyes dimmed. I sighed. Man is the only animal that feels remorse. This is why the vast majority of people prefer to let someone else kill their meat: so they don't have to look it in the eye, so they don't have to sigh.

That mallard was the link I needed. Would I be able to hold a mallard in my hand ten years from now? Would anyone be able to in one hundred? The best thing for the ducks would be if *everyone* went hunting. Then *everyone* would feel the marsh magic, know the thrill of ducks on the wing, hear the ripping silk as birds tumbled to set into the decoys. And *no one* would ever let anyone threaten that experience.

Judging from his broad breast, I knew I would find rich yellow fat beneath the mallard's skin. The bulging crop shifted, sounding like a bean-bag. It was thick with grain.

It is a common misconception that the migration moves only south. Many ducks travel at least as far east as they do south during their autumnal travels, and some travel west.

It is possible for a pintail duck born in Saskatchewan to winter south-west in California, or south into Louisiana, or even southeast in North Carolina. A blue-winged teal wintering in Venezuela may have flown there via New Brunswick or Maine after spending the summer in Manitoba, the first half of its intercontinental journey spent flying nearly due east from its prairie home.

I find this fact comforting. I certainly hadn't constrained myself to any particular direct-line itinerary, nor was I likely to. With the severe drought it was difficult to find water, and the key to my journey was not so much a hunt for ducks as a hunt for wet marshes. So far, I may have seen ducks that would end up in any of the four flyways.

I had been engaging, so far, in a "fall shuffle," similar to the movements of the ducks. During the period just before the fall migration takes place, ducks of the prairie-pothole region shuffle about in all directions. For example, birds from Minnesota may fly north to Manitoba to take advantage of a particular food source. I remember hearing about a hailstorm that had flattened some Manitoba wheat fields. It was useless for the farmers to attempt a harvest, so they left the grain where it lay. Ducks poured in to feast on the wheat. A great number of the birds, mallards mostly, wore leg bands indicating they were Minnesota ducks. I wonder how a Minnesota duck heard about Manitoba food.

When the morning grew long, the shadows short, and the coffee cold, I creaked out into the water to gather the decoys. Rascal had made two more retrieves: a fat gadwall drake and another greenhead lay with the first mallard in the duck blind. She sniffed them, wagging her tail. Exaltation. What did she smell?

I put my nose in one bird's downy breast. I could smell the damp duckweed in its feathers, along with the sweet, rank odor of duck that has always reminded me of freshly split, green birch. If one could smell time, he would do so in the breast feathers of a duck. Time to feed, time to fly far away, time to breed, time to die. Centuries lie musty in an unbroken cycle in a duck's breast. Ducks make ducks. Droughts come and go. Men and foxes kill and eat ducks. Pestilence decimates flocks. These things have always been, will always be. Ducks have every skill, every instinct, every tool that they need for survival. The myriad factors that have short-circuited their cycle revolve around a single hub: habitat. The lack of habitat diversity and changes in the face of the land have pushed the birds to new lows.

I packed up my hunting gear. Great wedges of snow geese strung out white against the new, blue sky above us, clamoring south. Rascal and I began the long walk back to the truck briskly beneath their music. The bur oaks rattled dead leaves in the stiff breeze. A cold front was moving through. Tomorrow we'd leave, blow into the Dakotas. I'd be looking for hope. Hope for me and for the ducks.

The bitter prairie wind died with the setting of the sun. For hours the camper's canvas had rattled as the chill wind whipped across the lake through the sparse barrier of trees. Dinner and the dishes done, sleep announcing its arrival through wide yawns, I flung the door open and stepped into the night.

Rascal bounded from the truck, rooting through the darkness while I stood still until my eyes adjusted. Overhead were brilliant stars and a cold white moon, nearly full, throwing faint shadows to the ground. The lake was silver in its light, and the wind-whipped white foam along its shore glistened like snow. The cold night air found its way down my neck. I turned my collar against it.

Away on the highway was the distant whining of truck tires. To the south, owls conversed, taking turns in an echoing discussion of territories, mice, and the hunt to come. Rascal ripped about in the dry leaves, burning energy to keep warm. As she ran, I felt as much as heard the evenly spaced stomping of a hoof, then a startled bawl. I found the whistle around my neck, and blew it. The dog has startled a deer. Rascal responded to the whistle's call as the deer crashed away through the brush.

In the moonlight, we paused on a knoll overlooking the lake. Aspen leaves rattled on the branches. Rascal stopped ten feet away and slightly above me. I could see that she was tense, her ears perked in attention. She slowly sank to her haunches. Eyes glaring, nose working, ears up, she pierced the night.

Straining to hear, it was minutes before I became aware of what it was that called her so. Denied to me by all my senses but one, I caught a clamor coming. From the west, across the lake, wafted the barking of snow geese, faintly at first and then building. They were flying very low.

It seemed strange to me that I could hear them so clearly and not be able to see them. They must have been very near, and yet no matter how I tried to focus on the barking, I could see nothing. I thought that this must be what it feels like to be blind. It was as if I were privy to the cavorting of spirits in the night.

Rascal again became my radar. I watched where she watched, turned my head as she turned hers. Soon she looked straight up. I followed her lead. The darkness was full of the sound of geese: joyful honking and even the sweeping of wind through feathers. How could I not see them, not see these ventriloquist geese throwing their voices? Then they flew beyond us, heading east. I spotted a small cloud, lit white by the moon. If only the geese would fly below it!

Child in the dark, I ran to another opening. I was lucky. The geese passed beneath the lone white cloud, and against its canvas I could see painted the uneven vee of two dozen snow geese, their direction unerring, wings beating slowly. Rowing across the breadth of the cloud, they disappeared into the darkness. Where were they going in the night?

The barking grew faint, then ceased. I felt somehow very successful because I was able to spot the geese, to prove to my eyes that my ears were not lying. I also felt very lucky to be here, standing with a wind on my neck, stars above, listening to the night talk of geese. Did anyone besides me hear these geese? I wanted to tell everyone else in the world to come outside, to stand perched in the darkness to wait for their geese to come—and to feel rich.

I buried my cold hands in my jacket pockets. Rascal was rooting again. I scuffed my feet through the drifts of leaves, like a child, thrilled at watching them swirl in the moonlight.

We rambled down to the lake. It was very cold. Perhaps that was why the geese were leaving. The small ponds would freeze again tonight, maybe to stay frozen until distant spring.

Rascal lapped noisily at the water, turned, and bit the foam until she developed a white beard. She looked pleased with herself. What a clown!

Turning toward the camper, I'm wrenched to a stop. From the west again came more goose music. A lone goose, following the same path as had the flock moments ago. Was it racing to catch them?

I cannot imitate a snow-goose bark, but I can do a respectable Canada-goose call. So I honked. The goose replied. When it was almost overhead, I honked again. I could hear it turn, hear the wind in pinions, hear the change of direction in its calling. We chatted. Was I asking it to come down, or was it imploring me to come with? When the goose came very near, its barking ceased. Then came some little grunts, disgusted little grunts as it discovered my falseness. It flew silently away.

I looked at the dog. She sat absolutely aquiver. I knew what she was thinking: "Just a little lower, boss. Just a little lower, and maybe I could have got it." Dogs are optimists, always. This is why we love them.

Cold leaked into my boots. I turned back to the camper, clapping Rascal to my side. I looked to see that all was stored safely and made sure that truck windows were rolled up and the cooler was tucked under the bumper. From inside the camper I heard the comforting hum of the furnace fan. Suddenly, I felt very tired. I opened the door and Rascal leaped in, climbed up on the seat, and flopped down on my hunting coat, happy.

Happy, too, I poured a scotch and opened a bag of Mary Jo's chocolate-chip cookies. Boots off, I propped my woolen feet before the heater. Scotch. Cookies. A snoring Labrador. Spirit snow geese in the night.

This ought to be illegal.

NORTH DAKOTA

Morris Nielsen is the king of the sneak hunters. Sneak hunting is the preferred method of hunting for many rural North Dakotans. No sitting in potholes over decoys for them. They would rather walk with the stiff wind at their backs or crawl on their bellies, hoping to surprise a flock of mallards loafing in the protective lee on some hidden pothole.

Of course, no one shoots anything but mallards here. All other ducks are "shit ducks." I cringe when I hear that term, but it is a common expression. Think of a dapper baldpate. Or a handsome pintail drake. How can they be shit ducks? But that's the way it is in North Dakota.

As I was saying, Morris is the king of the sneak hunters. Despite his size (a big Scandinavian wheat farmer) and the fact he won't walk one inch farther than necessary (a trait common across the western states, where with a pick-up truck you can drive on virtually any terrain), Morris has an uncanny knack for getting quietly into gun range of mallards and some-times geese.

Hunting this way is a bit too much like a trip to a meat market to appeal to me. (Granted, these "steaks" have a tendency to be nervous and pretty good at avoiding you.) But it fits the needs of the landowners who simply want to get a duck or two for dinner with a minimum of effort. I was along for the ride, staying for a few days with the Nielsens after wandering south from Manitoba.

Morris has lived on the Dakota prairie all his life. He and his son-in-law, Bruce Underdahl, raise wheat and sunflowers on the vast, flat fields southwest of Minot. They work very hard and have hearts as big as the prairie. These are truly fine people.

I have to tell you a story that shows just what these people are like. Fifteen years ago, my brother Butch and I were staying with the Nielsens when we first hunted in this area. One morning over coffee Butch remarked to one of their neighbors that we were headed for Watford City the next day to hunt pheasants.

"Where you going to stay?" the neighbor asked me.

"Oh, I dunno. Suppose we'll find a motel."

"There's only one and that will be full, it being the opening of the pheasant season and all. Tell you what, I got this big Winnebago in my Quonset hut. She's all gassed up and ready to go. The wife and I haven't used it since my heart attack last year, and it needs to be driven. Why don't you stop over later and pick it up?"

We protested. I mean, those things cost tens of thousands of dollars. I really didn't want the responsibility that came with borrowing it, but he wouldn't take no for an answer. So there you have it. Have you ever met someone who, ten minutes after meeting you, would lend you a thirty-thousand-dollar rig on a handshake? "Just fill up the tank when you bring it back."

Isn't that how it always is? I mean, I've been railing against the agricultural destruction of wildlife habitat, and I have a friend whose farm practices are probably not so very different. But I like Morris and Bruce and Morris's lovely wife, Wenona. Their farm is the picture of industry, and they are successful on the land. So I stopped by to do a little duck hunting with Morris.

Morris knows where every pothole, wet or dry, exists within a twenty-mile radius of his farm. We were driving cross-country, bouncing up and down hills and through gullies, often in a sea of tall grass, searching for a bit of wet in this agonizingly dry autumn. Morris eased the big pick-up up one of these hills, tall grass hissing on the truck's underside, the hood pointing briefly toward the sky as we reached the crest. When we could peek over the rise, he stopped the truck and let it roll quietly back down the hill for a few yards.

"Mallards," Morris whispered, turning off the ignition.

Morris, his grandson, Chris, and I eased out of the rig, shutting the doors quietly. Rascal and Morris's two black Labs whimpered in their dog crates in the bed of the truck. I watched as Chris and Morris loaded their shotguns, grandfather watching grandson to make sure the teenager was careful with his firearm. I trailed them as they crept up the rise.

Morris hunched his big frame over and moved his cowboy-booted feet carefully. Stopping short of the crest to avoid being "skylined" to the ducks, we knelt to reconnoiter.

Below lay a span of blue a half mile long. The valley in which it lay was steep-sided, and the whole wonderful place would be easy to miss if you happened to pass only a few hundred yards away. I marvel every time Morris shows me such a place, for each is so totally alive and so perfectly hidden. The earth seems to open up before you, and in a second, where there was nothing but rolling prairie, a vibrant oasis leaps into view. Miracles. Footprints of glaciers. Oh, how inviting they must look to ducks on the wing!

The Prairie Pothole

When the Wisconsin ice sheet of the last glacial period, about fifteen thousand years ago, retreated northward, it left in its wake tens of thousands of landlocked icebergs. They settled into the soil, and as they melted they became the foundation of the prairie pothole. An estimated ten million glacially carved depressions once pocked the landscape of the prairie-pothole region of the United States and Canada.

As the climate warmed, the ice melted and the fertile prairie pothole evolved, a habitat so lush that over 130 different bird species may use a single slough in one year. Seventy of those species will nest in or near that pothole.

Ducks probably pioneered into what is now the pothole region by extending their spring migration slowly northward as the climate

Morris and Chris decided on the best way to approach the ducks. Fifty or more mallards sat on or near the shore, about a hundred yards away. Crouching and sneaking, the two made off while I watched from the hill.

What I could see—but what they could not—was that the mallards already knew we were here. The birds began to walk into the water, slowly and with no sign of worry, before the two hunters had gone even halfway. By the time Morris and Chris approached the cattail-rimmed shore, the mallards were in a tight bunch, thirty yards out. By the time the men had reached the water's edge and stood up, guns ready, the ducks were launching into flight, the hundred flashing wings sounding like distant pounding on wood. Even the king of the sneak hunters doesn't always succeed.

When my two friends returned, we opened some cans of pop and watched the world from the silent hilltop. Rolling tan, brown, and gray hills flowed away to the northwest, each one crested like a wave, each one pointing down the path the glacier had left. As worn out as the description is, the prairie really does look like an ocean.

warmed. Prairie potholes and ducks are very well adapted to each other. Many ducks, because they are highly territorial, will not tolerate other ducks of the same species nesting nearby. With millions of potholes to choose from, ducks were easily able to disperse, each occupying its own nesting site. The diversity of potholes, ranging from small spring ponds to large permanent wetlands, provided the ducks with the various habitats necessary for each specific stage in their breeding and brood-rearing cycles.

Prairie potholes produce 50 percent of North America's ducks. The number of potholes has been rapidly decreasing as land is converted for agriculture. In North Dakota's prime pothole region, where up to one hundred wetland basins per square mile once existed, 60 percent of the original five million acres of wetlands have been lost. Ninety-five percent of that loss is attributable to agriculture. Only 1 percent of North Dakota's remaining wetlands are in public ownership.

Slate sky hung low over us. The wind blew clean and crisp over the grassland, hissing. Skeins of geese wiggled from the north. The mallards that we had disturbed came back in twos and threes, landing a safe distance offshore.

"Look at this crap," Morris said, sweeping his big hand across the sea of grass. "The government's paying us money to grow this stuff."

Morris was referring to the Conservation Reserve Program (CRP) land and payments, a program of the 1985 Farm Bill that paid farmers thirty to sixty-five dollars an acre to take erodable land out of production, seed it to cover, and set it aside for a decade.

Farmers do not see what I see when scanning this land. They see weeds, grass, and lost production on land that had taken great effort to free from the tight prairie sod, land that had grown bushels of wheat and sunflowers. They see neighbors leaving, and schools and churches and towns struggling to stay alive as the number of farmers decreases and the young people move away. Much of this decline is not the result of the CRP though. Today's intensive agriculture works best on big farms, and many fewer people are needed to work the land. But the CRP perhaps is seen as at least part of the problem.

As I looked around I saw something utterly different. I saw a great hope for the prairie wildlife. I saw wetlands with water despite the drought, while those potholes on farmed land were largely dry. The tall grass had held the meager snowfall so it could melt in place and flow downhill to the waiting wetlands. I saw nesting sites for ducks and other birds, lush meadows for deer, and untrammeled land for burrowing owls. I saw a bit of the past, mile after mile (there are three million acres of CRP land in North Dakota) of grassland that must look much like it did one hundred years ago. The wind was fresh; the topsoil did not drift like smoke in the breeze. And the water was pure; the wetlands were not inundated with agricultural chemicals.

"I'll tell you, Morris," I said, screwing up nerve enough to contradict my farmer friend, "as a taxpayer, I'd much rather have my dollars going into land for wildlife than into subsidizing someone to grow wheat we don't need."

He nodded. As if to show his willingness to consider this idea, he stated firmly, "You know, while plowing or haying I've moved the nests of more ducks than I've ever shot. We farmers talk about that at the coffee shop, wherever, 'How many nests did you move today?'"

As we talked, a flock of Canada geese cried their way from the north. Against a patch of blue in the otherwise gray sky, they turned. Obviously, they had seen something they liked. The leader headed down, black wings pumping and dark legs outstretched. With a single mind, the flock twisted, responded, and mimicked the leader. In a moment, one hundred geese had landed on a hilltop half a mile away. Sentries patrolled, their long necks silhouetted against the sky, while the remaining birds fed.

"Those are the big fellas, the big honkers," Morris said, looking at them through binoculars. "Oh, if it were windier, I could sneak them."

I chuckled. King of the sneak hunters.

Back in the pick-up, we drove on. I was startled by the change in the land since I had been here two years ago. Grass on thousands of acres of CRP land waved on the hills. What in 1987 had been mostly badly eroded, barren hillsides turned fallow to the winter wind were now locked tight in grass. As we traveled on, slowly driving old prairie trails, a group of antelope startled from the grass, flowing on fluid legs down a valley beneath us and over a hill. The buck stopped and looked back at us, his tawny form outlined on the skyline, his white rump hairs erected in a brilliant warning flag to every antelope within sight. Before we had gone much farther, a pair of white-tailed deer leaped from the ditch and raced the truck for half a mile, bounding in great graceful arcs in the late afternoon sun. Chris, Morris, and I watched, our faces split with smiles. I do not know what Morris was thinking, but I felt that this display of wildlife was worth every penny the government had spent. What price can you put on such enrichment? How much more pleasurable to live in a land that is alive!

The prairie, given a chance, had revived in two years. True, this was not the native prairie. The native prairie would have been made up of tall and short grass types, such as wheatgrass, bluestem, cordgrass, and buffalo grass. In spring, the prairie would have been green. In summer, it would have burst with color as showy forbs peeked through the bluestem sod. And in the autumn, the landscape would have been awash with gray, silver, purple, and copper. Most of this domesticated grass would in a short time mat down and be somewhat less useful to wildlife. But this alternative was far better than intensive agriculture.

As we watched the antelope and deer run wild on the plains, I thought how magnificent it would have been to have seen this place before the coming of the white man. Think of the great, pounding herds of buffalo streaming through the grass. Sense the earth shudder, smell the dust on the wind, feel it lie gritty on your sweaty neck, hear the great groaning and grunting as thousands of gigantic mammals flow by in a living stream. In their grazing and wandering, huge herds practiced a natural "deferred" rotation, nipping the prairie and fertilizing it at the same time, then moving on, not to return until it was lush again. Antelope fed on the forbs the bison disdained. Elks split the rolling hills with their eerie mating bugle. Prairie wolves worried the herds, picking off stragglers. The great plains grizzly lumbered along cottonwood river bottoms, looking for meat. The panoply was lush, a great mosaic of green grass, millions of mammals, sky dark with the rush of wings. Ever moving, ever changing, evolving, blood, dust, birth, death, all entwined.

There is, in my estimation, a sinister criminality to what we did to the prairie. I am reminded of the current uproar about the demise of African wildlife, through destruction of habitat and slaughter by poachers, across that continent's great grasslands. What hypocrisy we practice! We have not saved a place on the North American prairie where life can continue as it evolved, where life can continue to evolve.

In a period of less than one hundred years we have tamed a land once as wild and lush as the Serengeti Plain of Africa. Sixty million buffalo were slaughtered in three years, not to meet a need, but to forever destroy the life-style of the Plains Indians and to open the land for agriculture and cattle. The destruction of the last prairie potholes, and the ducks that symbolize them, is merely an extension, though less bloody, of that laying to waste of an entire ecosystem.

Wherever farming occurs, the prairie has been altered completely. I accept that. There is nothing wrong or dishonorable about farming. Farming is essential to our culture and the people who work the land to raise our food should do so with pride.

What *is* wrong is not saving some bits and pieces for wildlife and plants. What is incredibly criminal is draining even one more wetland in the face of what we know. And our society, which fosters these destructive practices through subsidies that encourage erosion, pollution, and habitat loss, is an accomplice to the crime. Many of these programs put money in the pockets of farmers who simply aren't good enough to be farmers.

Subsidies depend on the farm producer's base acreage. They therefore encourage fencerow to fencerow planting in order to increase that base. The programs actually penalize those landowners who leave windbreaks and wetlands untouched since they can't include this "unproductive" land in their base. In recent years, commodity programs have cost the American taxpayer up to twenty-five billion dollars annually.

The public is also paying for needed water treatment, increased dredging on waterways, silted reservoirs, and lost recreational opportunities—all of which are directly attributable to the cropping of erosive soils.

Good farmers will make it on the land. Sixty percent of American farmers do not ask for, or benefit by, the handouts. Even during the worst of the farm crisis of the 1980s, the farm failure rate was far below any other business venture. In 1987, the average net income of a full-time farmer was just over one hundred thousand dollars per year.

Yet, in that same year, more than seven hundred million dollars in federal farm subsidies was paid out in North Dakota alone. The state's total population, farmers and city dwellers alike, is about seven hundred thou-

◄ Saskatchewan's Quill
Lakes are a major
staging area for tens
of thousands of geese
and ducks.

Saskatchewan's park-
land regions have
largely been converted
to agriculture.
Migrating geese and
cranes feed exten-
sively on the area's
▼ waste grain.

▲ Mallards staging on the Quill Lakes often fly in large flocks to feed in nearby wheat stubble fields. Agriculture and drought have reduced Saskatchewan's mallard production from its traditional five million birds per year to only one million.

Manitoba's ► October skies fill with huge flocks of migrating snow geese. Because their Arctic habitat has not yet felt the encroachment of man, snow geese numbers have been growing.

▲ Across Manitoba, and indeed throughout the prairie pothole region, farmers took advantage of the drought to burn, then plow, many of the remaining wetlands.

Rascal retrieves a ► drake wigeon in an icy Turtle Mountain lake. The many lakes of Manitoba's Turtle Mountain Park provide the more drought resistant wetlands so important to migrating ducks.

◄ A decade of drought left this North Dakota pothole like thousands of others across the prairie, dry and cracked. Although drought actually helps recharge a wetland's nutrients, many farmers used this period to convert potholes to cropland.

Over fifty percent of North Dakota's prairie wetlands has been lost, most to agriculture. Remaining wetlands are low in waterfowl pro-
▼ duction, but still play an important role in the birds' migration.

◄ Canada geese descend into a southern cypress forest in December. Seasonally flooded habitats like this have dwindled because of flood-control efforts.

The end of the migration is the Gulf Coast. Carved up with oil company canals and denied renewing Mississippi River water, the coastal ▼ marshes are becoming saline and eroding.

sand. The taxpayers of this nation should expect more than wasted topsoil, polluted waters, and devastated wildlife populations for their dollars.

The somber skies grew ever darker. We continued down back roads, stopping at spots that looked indistinguishable from the rest of the terrain but that inevitably held potholes. Most of the potholes were dry, but occasionally one would sparkle with wetness.

Finally, Morris and Chris executed a successful sneak. When they had crept to the edge of the cattails, the sky was shielded quickly with flashing wings, mallards leaping to the sky with the wind at their backs. From where I watched I could hear the strangely muffled *pop-pop-pop* of shotguns.

Morris waved. I let Rascal loose. She had some work to do.

First you look for the abandoned farm with the long, white, many-stalled outbuilding. Just before you reach it, turn right off the gravel road and onto a narrower, rutted dirt trail. Go past the small pothole on your left (where in the past I've seen dozens of mallards feeding) until you come to a rise. Now you are getting near.

Before long, you'll pass an empty farmhouse, this one only recently boarded up. There is a hill behind the farmhouse, and behind the hill, a half mile from the house, romp rolling hills that are dotted with potholes. These are big potholes, some of them stretching for a half a mile. This land is really too hilly to farm, although someone tried anyway. This is a place where topsoil blew in the wind, where rain guttered the fallow hillsides, and where ambitions and hopes became as fruitless as the land. Now this land, retired, is in grassy CRP.

From the crest of the hill I looked out over the valley beyond. The road, almost overgrown with grass, splits the wetlands into two enormous potholes. Then the trail climbs quickly to the top of the next steep hill. I don't know what is beyond.

This is a pilgrimage of sorts. I have been here in wetter years to hunt ducks, and it is a special place to me. As we bounced along, Rascal made noseprints on the windshield. In her excitement, she sniffed the air coming through the vents until they too were wet and shiny like her nose.

I had hoped to camp next to the slough so that I could go to sleep with the sound of the ducks' chortling feeding grunts in my ears, but the potholes were dry. In the middle of the easternmost pothole, though, there was a dark, moist spot, a brown stain the size of a house in the midst of the white, bitter soil. That was it?

We limped the truck slowly down the hill, driving now in the one-time wheat fields, unable to see anything but grass to the top of the hood. I hoped there were no big holes I might drop into unexpectedly. We stopped near a spartan rim of stunted cattails and got out.

Rascal quickly flushed a monster amongst grasshoppers, one easily as big as your thumb, that startled her as it whizzed past her nose. She jumped back, recovered, pounced on it like a cat would, and saw it squirt, clicking, from between her paws and sail into the cattails.

There is a big tree on the east end of the pothole, one lonely tree. I think it is a cottonwood. There was a hawk perched in the tree and when it saw us, it leaped to wing, stroked into the cold blue sky, and then began to soar in small, tight circles. In just a few minutes it gained altitude and became a mere speck. Perhaps it hoped that we'd startle a big jackrabbit from hiding so it could fall like a taloned stone from the sky to pounce upon it.

In the breast pocket of my hunting coat was the reason I had journeyed here. I pulled out a film canister. The contents rattled softly. I clenched the canister in my right hand and walked out into the pothole.

Two years ago, this pothole was full of water, the bottom so soft that you dared not stop while putting out the decoys or you'd sink out of sight. The shoreline cattails, now only knee-high, had been above my head. Now the pothole's bottom was so white and hard that you could drive an eighteen-wheeler across it. Cracks wide enough to put your hand in edgeways laced the surface. The land was as chapped as a Bedouin's face.

Two years ago, ducks fed and swam and rested here. Two years ago, I sat in the tall cattails as mallards circled warily and as green-winged teal ripped erratically across the gray water. Two years ago, I watched as wave after wave of sandhill cranes raced before the winter winds. And two years ago, the best friend I had ever had was with me, sitting beside me. The black-and-gray film canister held some of the ashes of that dear friend, and I had come to put her to rest.

Gypsy had been a black Labrador. She was fierce and gentle, loving and aloof. She had granted me her devotion, but I do not think I was ever her master. There was about her the air of utmost confidence; I knew that if she had ever wanted to leave me she would do so. Hers was not a puppyhood of love and affection. She had been abandoned and for months had run wild in the woods of northern Wisconsin. I know that she had hunted with, or at least encountered, the wild dogs, the coyotes, for she reacted to the song of wolves or coyotes with a deep, primordial reply. There was fire in her eyes.

She had ended up in a dog pound, and on the very day that she was to be destroyed, my father and I took her home. She was mangy, skinny, and, oh, so very happy. I think she had smelled the death in that place and knew what we had done for her. She was about a year old and, with food and care, came to be as beautiful a Labrador as ever lived.

The pothole on whose parched surface we stood was the pothole in which Gypsy had made her last retrieve. It was out last great hunt together, and I knew it. Maybe she did too. Though her heart beat with passion and her eyes watched the skies, her legs and hips were unsure, stiff. And when the mallards *flumped* at the sound of gunfire into the ice-skimmed pothole, she entered the water with the movement of an otter, not leaping, but slipping. We watched (my brother-in-law Bill was with me) nervously as the thirteen-year-old dog broke ice for fifty yards, thrashing it to shards to fetch our birds. I'll never forget the short, whistling gasps of her breathing as she struggled.

When she returned with the second bird, visibly worn, I looked deep into her eyes and saw a pain that I had never seen before: the pain of ambition that outstripped ability. I knew that she was doing what she loved most for the last time. And I cried.

It is a good thing that cattails are tall. Bill could not see me. I stroked Gypsy while her head rested on my lap and her wet hips quivered with the exertion. I whispered that I loved her, thanked her for all the pleasure she had given me, and told her she was a good dog. She searched my moist eyes, hers glinting with the fire that had always been there, piercing the pain. She said to me (as plainly as if she had voice) that she loved me and was glad, despite the pain, that she was here with me to retrieve my ducks. Oh, God, I sobbed, and hugged her.

A year later she was gone. She died in early autumn, days before duck season, claimed by a cancer that ate her insides. I watched her fail for a week before I could screw up the courage to take her in to the veterinarian. As I held her head on the cold steel table, crying but not caring who saw, I watched the needle slip into her vein. When she shuddered with death, she was breathing deeply through a duck wing I held before her nose.

She was my friend. She represented my youth. She had even saved my life once, swimming out to me as I floundered in a wild trout stream. I had tripped and my chest waders filled with icy April water. When I gasped to the surface for the third time I saw her otter head plowing water to me. I grabbed her, and holding on, was able to struggle to shore. She had a huge steak for dinner that evening.

So Rascal and I had come to this pothole to put her ashes to rest in a place that she loved, in a place where ducks would whistle over her head. I could see her vibrate at the sound, her brown eyes straining skyward.

I felt cheated. Cheated that she did not live to take this dream trip with me. Cheated that the pothole was dry. Cheated that the ducks would not come this year. I could not leave her in this desert, in this place forsaken by rain and wings.

I put the container back in my pocket. Rascal ran up to me, a goofy, happy look on her face. Gypsy was stately, a queen. Rascal is a court jester. I knelt down on the chalky soil and hugged Rascal tightly, putting my nose deep in her fur and sniffing her oily Labrador scent. I had seen her heart when she fought ice in Manitoba. I had watched her learn to scan the sky for birds. She was my friend. She would represent my middle age.

With Rascal at my side and Gypsy in my pocket, I walked back to the truck. Gypsy would finish the trip with me.

The threat of cold weather that had driven the ducks, Rascal, and me out of Manitoba had given way to a week of warm, almost hot, prairie days. The mornings would dawn crisply, but by afternoon, blue skies let the sun warm the land and melt any ice. It appeared that for the time being migration had halted and the birds were enjoying the fruits of autumn before moving on.

Although agricultural practices have devastated the nesting grounds of prairie ducks, it has at least provided them with a wealth of food in the form of waste grain. Because of this food supply, and as long as there is water on which to rest, many species of waterfowl, especially mallards and geese, linger in the north. Once the potholes freeze, the flocks move to larger, ice-free bodies of water. Only when snow cover prevents access to food will they move south.

I don't suppose that days of the week mean much to ducks; they certainly mean little to me as I travel with them. Mondays are much like

Tuesdays, which are much like Fridays. But today is Sunday. I know it because as I wander through the Coteau country, through the running hills and past the farms and small towns, I see the trucks and cars nuzzled around the prairie churches like cows at a trough.

I also know it is Sunday by the fresh-scrubbed faces in every vehicle I pass on the straight Dakota roads. (Farm country is neatly laid out in one-mile grids along which the roads run, the better to sift the wealth of the land.)

Try this if you ever go to North Dakota. Try to wave *before* the driver of the oncoming vehicle does. You simply can't. Trying is like being in a gunfight. The fastest wave in the West. Of all the places I have been to date, North Dakota is the friendliest, topping even Manitoba by five waves to two.

These are not boisterous, arm-out-the-window waves. Usually, half a hand—fingers only—is lifted above where it rests on the top of the steering wheel, almost in a Boy Scout salute. No doubt the gesture evolved from genuine gladness in seeing someone else on the wide expanse of the prairie. Friendliness goes to the heart of these people. They have not been contaminated by the cynicism of our time. Even women wave, alone in their cars. Can you imagine urban women waving at men they do not know?

Yet when I see these good people strolling out of the church to talk to each other and to shake the minister's hand, I wish that the love they share for each other and their God would also extend to the land. Each of us is responsible for the earth, and we must examine the beliefs and philosophies that have turned our culture against it.

Western civilization, with its primarily Christian philosophy, has put man at odds with nature. Christianity establishes that man is here to dominate all other life forms, having been created in the image of God. (How convenient! You have to wonder who thought that up.) Man is placed at the top of the ladder, which is only correct if you envisage mankind on the top rung of responsibility, not rights. What this philosophy ignores is that man is not the center of the web of life, but is as dependent on every other strand as is all other life.

Christianity also tells us to "be fruitful and multiply," as if the ability to reproduce were a badge of distinction. Today it is simply irresponsible to allow human populations to grow unchecked, giving no consideration to the needs of the planet. Overpopulation condemns most of humanity to lives of poverty, hopelessness, and ugliness as the world continues to erode.

Theologians bemoan secular society for being human-centered. Yet Christianity itself is human-centered. Is it a joy in the eyes of God to see a wetland drained, a river polluted? Do these things honor God? His work? Yet Christians encourage conversion of the land for the good of man.

Christianity allows the beasts no soul. Yet each creature has a spirit of sorts, which was known by other cultures, such as the American Indians. They would ask for each creature's understanding when they took its life, knowing that as the animal must take lives to foster its life, so must man. There was a sense of oneness with the land, and the natural community was allowed a sense of dignity that has been lost since we've reduced the natural world to a commodity.

Aldo Leopold said it best: "A land ethic changes the role of *Homo sapiens* from conqueror of the land-community to plain member and citizen of it." Religion seems to encourage ethical treatment of other people, but not to allow the extension of those ethics to the land. To do so would be to admit that the land and the animals on it also have a right to ethical treatment, a thought that human-centered religion will not abide. If for no other reason than to maintain its strictly human-centered philosophy without wavering, Christianity should begin preaching conservation . . . or there will be no humanity to serve.

At the opposite end of the scale are groups so completely separated from how nature truly works that they are opposed to the use of any animal product. Ethical treatment of nature recognizes our rights to exist and to use the land, as well as the rights of the rest of the land-community to their places in the system; it acknowledges that all life is interwoven. There is nothing evil about eating another creature. The wolf feels no guilt, neither should man. When all members of the biotic community operate as they should, without greed or malice, the intricate lacework of life is safe from all but cataclysmic disasters. And even these, one might argue, are part of the natural order.

There is a middle ground. One can be a Christian and still have a land ethic, for both are tapped by a common root: disdain for human pride.

Recognizing that we must extend an ethical code to our judgments about using natural resources is the only real hope for the environment. Only when we extend the boundaries of our consciences to include the land and all that is upon it will there be any meaningful change for the better.

In other words, unless society as a whole chastises the drainer and the developer, and unless a sense of guilt rides in the tractor cab with the farmer contemplating ruining a wetland, we will fail. We must use while not abusing.

Better Moses had come down from the mountain with an eleventh commandment: Thou shalt not covet the homes of thy fellow creatures nor lay waste to the land.

I have stayed on in North Dakota for three reasons: the ducks (and cranes and geese), the very fine people, and Harry's Diner in Medina.

At Harry's Diner, catty-corner across the wide main street of Medina from the bank, you can get a huge meal for $3.18, the kind of meal you need only eat once a day. Mashed potatoes and gravy, turkey or beef, vegetables—all like Mom made. Pudding comes with it, coffee too.

I like sitting at the 1950s-style counter. I don't take one of the few tables that I believe are probably "reserved" for the regulars in seed hats. Why upset the natural order of things? Also, everyone talks to the server behind the counter, so I can eavesdrop on conversations about the price of grain, the weather, and local news. I'd pay the three dollars just for the news; the meal's a bonus.

I've also hung around to pursue some upland game: pheasant, sharp-tailed grouse, and gray partridge. I'll need to pay bills when I get home, so I hunt and photograph in hopes of gathering material for articles.

Ron Stromstad told me about the diner. He knows them all. Ron is one of "them damn wildlifers," as some Dakota residents call people who work for the U.S. Fish and Wildlife Service. He is a big, sandy-haired, bespectacled North Dakota farm-boy-turned-biologist who has been breaking new ground in his home state (actually, putting old ground back into habitat) by convincing farmers and ranchers to make room for wildlife on their land. As a native son, he has a rapport with them that no bureaucrat could ever master. Ron optimistically told me, "The good conservation work will be done around the kitchen tables of North Dakota, over coffee and sweet rolls."

If prairie wildlife has anything going for it it is people like Stromstad. Enthusiasm is not something he is lacking, nor vision. You can't beat it: enthusiasm, hope, birds, and Harry's Diner.

Ron picked me up one day in his rattly government truck. (Rascal was granted special government dispensation to ride along.) He was determined to show me the cause for his optimism, and I needed a transfusion of hope. Ron's important program revolves around the simple premise (hooray!) that agriculture and wildlife can coexist, even prosper, but that land stewardship is the only way that both will survive. As we drove along, he freely quoted Aldo Leopold. Thank God for Aldo.

"I'm a firm believer that every tool we've got that can put a bird in the air had better be applied now," Ron said as we drove along, the wheat fields a tawny blur along the expressway. "Listen, we can't afford to lose this battle. We won't have another chance. If we win, the land and the people who live on it will all be healthier."

The hair on the back of my neck stood up. These are almost the exact words of Ross Melinchuk in Saskatchewan.

Heading north of the interstate, Ron slowed to a stop, checked a plat book, turned west, opened a gate, and drove into a pasture. The change in landscape was startling. A flock of sharp-tailed grouse erupted from the weathered grass. Beyond them we could see the lush green of a wetland. Ducks jumped for the sky when they heard the truck coming.

North Dakota Wildlife Extension Program

The North Dakota Wildlife Extension Program, developed in 1987, was designed to improve waterfowl production on private lands. The program, sponsored by the U.S. Fish and Wildlife Service, provides financial incentives and technical assistance to participating landowners. Wildlife biologists and farmers work together to create waterfowl habitat on marginal cropland.

In some instances the landowner allows the Service to manage Conservation Reserve Program acres for wildlife in exchange for an annual compensation of $5 per acre. (CRP lands are those that have been taken out of production to protect erodable soils.) Nesting habi-

"This is Frank Redlin's land. He's one of the best landowners enrolled in our program. Look at this pasture, the good condition, even during this drought. Forbs, flowers, all over the place. I tell you, if all the farmers in North Dakota were like this one, I'd be out of business."

"Using this twice deferred rotation grazing," Ron continued, sweeping his arm out over the pasture, "we've helped Frank increase his beef production and helped the wildlife, too."

"We've got seven million acres of grassland in North Dakota in desperate need of management," he said, emotion building in his tone. "If we could get even one million acres into rotational grazing . . ." As he spoke, his eyes lit up.

Quietly now, Ron continued. "It has to be long-term optimism. Ducks still lay eggs and they do it one at a time. We lost our wetlands one at a time. And that's the only way we're going to get it back: one step at a time."

The twists and turns left me wondering where we were. Finally, a landmark: the tiny town of Robinson. We were nearing the infamous dog-vomit campsite near Chase Lake.

I'd been drinking Thermos coffee all morning and as Ron once again turned off a road onto a prairie trail, the truck did painful things to my

---

tat is created through financial incentives to set aside land from agriculture for up to ten years. The average cost for these agreements is $5.50 per acre. The program also encourages wetland restoration by compensating farmers' costs to plug drainage ditches on farm property and by paying a cash bonus of $10 per wetland acre.

Thousands of nests and young birds of all types are saved by delaying haying on productive nesting areas. To compensate farmers for a reduction in yield or quality when haying is delayed until after the hatch, the program pays $4.60 per acre. Farmers are also encouraged to install nesting structures and to place predator-control fences around nesting habitat.

Helping landowners to modify grazing systems or tillage operations has proven to increase agricultural yields and reduce soil erosion. It is also an inexpensive means of increasing wildlife production on private lands. The extension program provides educational information, technical advice, and fencing materials to participating farmers and ranchers.

bladder. A few cattle grazed across a fence running parallel to our path. Rascal gave them an ominous throaty growl of warning. Ron and I laughed. Rascal has growled at cattle ever since she startled a moose (or a moose startled her) on a portage trail in the Minnesota lakeland wilderness. She seems to think cattle are moose.

A ring of dusty, battered pick-up trucks were herded near the end of the trail, behind a closed gate. We stopped, and Rascal and I watered the prairie. (There is little discretion on the prairie for there is little to hide behind. You just turn your back, and everyone else pretends not to notice.) I put her back in the truck, and we walked on.

A cool northwest wind was at our backs. Wisps of white clouds ripped along in the breeze, streaking the robin's-egg blue sky. I liked the way the grass bowed in the wind, hissing.

"This is great," Ron said. "Wait till you see these guys. This is a perfect example of the changes we're seeing here. I warn you, though, they won't be very talkative."

Seven men strained on the grassland, stretching an electric fence. A farm tractor hummed nearby, equipped with a post-hole digger. We had walked out onto a beaten peninsula, a moonscape of cow pies and abused turf. The peninsula measured about twenty-five acres and thumbed its way out into a giant pothole. Even the cattails along the edge of the water had been stomped into dust by the cows.

"What we're doing here," Ron explained, "is creating an artificial island by putting a predator-proof fence across the base of the peninsula. When that's done and when the grass grows back and the drought ends, the ducks and shorebirds will have a safe nesting area."

He went on to say that studies have shown that on natural islands, ducks have sometimes achieved a 90 percent success rate when nesting, far above the 10 to 15 percent rate now common on the predator-infested prairie. It was hoped that the ducks that nested on this peninsula would mimic that success. The fence going up right before our eyes was a beautiful sight because of who was putting it up, and why. I asked one farmer why they were laboring so for wildlife. "'Cause Ron asked us," he replied. If only solutions were always that easy.

"That's Levi Patzner. He's been restoring wetlands all over his property and on many of his neighbors'. Has his tractor all set up for the work. He's also put nesting structures out all over hell. You should talk to him." Ron glowed as we walked over to shake hands.

So I asked Levi the obvious question: Why had they taken such a dramatic turn from their recent past of wetland destruction? "Because I like wildlife," he replied uncomfortably before turning back to his work.

I photographed the fence crew and then walked to the end of the peninsula, envisaging the day when water would lap at its rim, tall grass having returned, and ducks would waddle their broods down to feed in the fertile pothole. When I returned, Levi was looking for me.

"Been thinking of what you asked," he said quietly, rubbing a chapped hand on his chin's gray stubble. "I've got a lot of land in CRP that I can't raise grain on. I might as well raise wildlife on it. I'd like to see some of the habitat come back so it's ready when the drought ends. I remember what it used to be like, when we saw lots of ducks and grouse all the time. I'd like to leave something behind when I'm gone."

He turned, started to walk away, stopped and looked me square in the eye. "There's been just an awful lot of potholes drained in my time. An awful lot." He was searching for more words. "Look, a lot of this land should have never been broken anyway. Farmers knew that. The soil's too light. But the government paid us," he said with feeling. "What the hell do we want to raise wheat on this land for, anyway?"

You could have knocked me over with a feather. I shook Levi's hand again, thanking him. I hope he knew that I was thanking him for restoring not only the land, but my faith and hope. There was room for optimism.

We said goodbye to the fence crew. Everyone joked with Ron, although you could tell they were uneasy with this new friendship with the "damn wildlifers." But they were also proud of what they were doing. More than the habitat was being restored: Ron had spawned a new relationship with the people of the prairie, an essential, overdue relationship.

"What'd I tell you," Ron said in a proud-father voice as we walked back to the truck. "One step at a time."

My God, I thought, this man is going to have to eat a silo-full of sweet rolls and drink a pothole-full of coffee.

A lot of my days are spent in rather aimless wandering, looking for food, water, a shower, and a place to rest for the night. I'm like the ducks, except for the shower. You can't travel that much without seeing something, each day, that is noteworthy.

Item: On the hot blacktop of Highway 36, between the tiny town of Wilton and the even smaller burg of Wing, a highway-department employee has had some fun with asphalt sealer. It is an odd design, a duck drawn as big as a car, a beautiful mallard taking wing, traced in black goo on an asphalt canvas. Who is this Michelangelo of North Dakota? Think of the heart it took to do that on a blistering summer day while trying to avoid detection by the supervisor and while orange safety cones squeezed traffic until the masterpiece dried. Thanks.

Item: We are camped on the bluffs above Lake Sakakawea, North Dakota's "great lake," on the Missouri River. I am answering an urgent call of nature at about four in the morning. A nearly full moon casts empty shadows on the prairie. But there is something else: a green glow. Northern lights ripple across the sky like velvet curtains. The moon, which has burned a hole through them, is ringed in concentric celadon halos, each bigger than the next. A bull's-eye.

Item: Daybreak in a pothole. Rascal is perched on a mansion of a muskrat house, and I am standing almost chest-deep in the ooze and water

Prairie Predators

Predators have always existed on the prairie. In recent times, however, both the numbers and the species found there have increased, posing a serious threat to many ground-nesting birds, including ducks.

Agriculture has changed the ecosystem to the benefit of predator species. Crows, with their insatiable taste for eggs, have expanded north and west. Abandoned farms, ditches, rock piles, and waste grain provide den sites and food for raccoons, which are increasing in number and range throughout the prairie. Skunks have multiplied as well. All feed extensively upon the eggs of ground-nesting birds such as ducks, grouse, plover, and many songbirds. In addition, limited nesting cover places all birds in close proximity to predators.

Fox populations, always a part of the prairie ecosystem, have exploded because of the elimination of the prairie wolf and the connext to it. Ice coats everything, including the dog, who had to swim in the dark to her hiding place. My hands are so cold that they hurt and have quit working. Rascal's teeth chatter, her face suddenly aged with white, frosty fur, eyelashes glittering. The muskrat swims by, looks annoyed, and dives. I can see it swimming underwater. Do muskrats bite?

The decoys are frozen in place. Ducks laugh at us as they pass, sail far down the pothole, land, and chuckle. From behind us comes the tremolo of cranes. They come with the dawn, first in twos and threes, then in tens and twenties. They are flying so low that they barely clear the few willows on the pothole's rim, so low that I could have knocked them down with a pole, so low that when they row by I can hear the swishing of their feathered oars, so low that I can watch as their long necks and even longer legs undulate in alternate rhythm with their wingbeats. Red-crested heads turn this way and that. They utter a wild cry, filling the air and our ears.

Rascal watches with me, enchanted. The sandhill cranes fly by in wave after wave. An hour passes before the last crane does.

The ducks are still laughing when we leave.

---

trol of the coyote population. Wolves kept the coyotes in check and coyotes limited fox numbers within their territories. This natural interspecies competition evolved into a system that favored large carnivores and limited smaller egg- and bird-eating predators. Researchers estimate that there are now 250,000 foxes in North Dakota alone. They say this number must be reduced by half in order to ensure the future for ground-nesting birds.

Complicating the scenario are the animal rights activists. Through their efforts they have cut fur prices, and thus trapping, the only feasible method to reduce predator numbers on the out-of-balance prairie.

Across the prairie-pothole region, some two hundred million duck eggs (and 20 percent of the hens) are destroyed by predators each year. Only one in ten nesting duck hens now produces a brood, down from four in ten in the last few decades. Seventy percent of those losses are attributable to predation. Some areas are experiencing duck nest success as low as 8 percent. To remain stable, a population of ducks needs a 20 percent success rate.

Item: Red foxes are everywhere. Raccoons and skunks, too. Mostly you see them mashed on the roadside. Sometimes you see foxes running, red streaks in the grass. Skunks you hope you don't see, especially a foot in front of your dog, tail raised.

I have conflicting emotions. I love to watch the foxes. They are beautiful. But they eat ducks, as do skunks and raccoons. So I cheer all the roadkills.

As we watch one ruddy fox lope gracefully on the prairie Ron Stromstad says, "Look at that sonofabitch." Then he reflects, "I like foxes, I really do. They're beautiful critters. I just don't like seeing five or six per square mile."

Item: Woodworth, North Dakota. Ron pulls the truck into a driveway. There is an old, green duck boat parked on a trailer. We stop to pick up Leo Kirsch, an old man whose seriously poor health hasn't dampened his lust for waterfowl. Born on the prairie, he will probably die there among the ducks and geese and cranes and shorebirds that are his life and his work. Leo is a biologist, a retired National Wildlife Refuge manager.

Leo is slow-talking and deliberate. His is a gravelly voice that begs to be listened to. His wife bundles him up in enough clothing to survive the arctic, and he goes for a drive with us, binoculars dangling on his chest.

Leo is a kindred spirit. Ron chuckles as he tells this story:

"A young manager once asked Leo for advice on how to manage a refuge's grassland. Leo sent a sheet of paper back with five stick matches taped to it. The only thing written on it was 'Five Year Management Plan.'"

It's an inside joke. Refuges are often hayed or grazed, something that is controversial, especially with Leo. Wildfire is nature's way of renewing grassland, and some biologists believe in mimicking that process. Two things stop them: official policy (hay is valuable) and ignorance (fire is bad).

Leo's not bashful. He knew that I had come to hear about the prairie from someone who had the perspective of many years.

Leo spoke slowly, quietly as he remembered his youth on the Minnesota prairie: "You could go outside at recess in autumn during the worst part of the drought of the '30s and count flock after flock after flock of ducks. I don't know, you might see a dozen, fifteen big flocks of ducks all at once. You never see them migrating like that anymore. I haven't seen mass migrations since the '50s. They mustn't be there if you don't see them. I'm convinced that ducks were never in as much trouble in the '30s as they are now.

"Problem is, even if the drought ends, the ducks may not bounce back. The rest of the habitat is just not there, and the predators are so much worse. There were no raccoons back then."

Then, very upbeat, he said, "How'd you young fellas like to see more damn canvasbacks than you've ever seen in your life? Drive. I'll show you."

A thousand twists and turns past abandoned farms and stubble fields brought us to an area where grass and water still reigned. From a hillside, a flock of Canada geese lifted in a great clamor, swung into the wind, and passed very near the truck.

"Oh sure, now you see them. I went hunting for geese the other morning," said Leo (as I marveled at the thought of this frail old man slogging through a marsh in the dark). "Had visions of coming home with a white-front and a Canada. Hell, all I came home with was a wet butt."

He was excited, his old eyes peering through his binoculars at the swirling geese. "Them ain't those little grunts, either. They're the big grunts. Now that's an eatin' bird!"

Later, we crested a rise beyond which was a sea of grass and the emaciated body of a prairie lake. Leo was in his element. Every sight triggered a memory.

"This is famous South Lake. Old Doc Melzer delivered a baby some-where nearby in the '20s, then stopped and shot sixty-one canvasbacks here. A homesteader told me that in the old days he could hear the roar of ducks getting off the water two miles away."

Perspective. I don't even know what the sight of lots of ducks really is.

The truck clattered down a grass-choked trail, dust rising to creep in through the windows, coating everything and leaving a bitter taste on my lips. Over another rise there is more water, hard-stemmed bullrushes ring-ing it in.

A silver squadron lay at rest: bull canvasbacks en masse keeping to an ancient schedule. Other prairie ducks play hide-and-seek with the coming winter. Canvasbacks of the prairie have an internal clock, depart on a schedule as formal as a calendar. Having spent the late summer molting together on large sloughs, these migration flocks often consist largely of drakes. They leave the marshes of Manitoba during the second week of October. The cans and I had somehow arrived at this slough at the same time.

"Look at that, boys," Leo chimed, "there's six thousand canvasbacks sittin' out there."

We all watched the great gray-backed birds through binoculars. Small groups would get up to stretch their wings, run on the blue waters to gain speed, and lift on the wind to circle the lake. When they turned to the sun, they flashed like mirrors. So bright, it hurt my eyes, robbed my breath. Then, tilting downward, they would tear toward the water and gently set down, their leathery landing gear skiing to a stop.

"I'll wager, guys, that within seven miles of where we're standing there are fifteen thousand canvasbacks," Leo said, binoculars to his eyes.

There are somewhat fewer than five hundred thousand of these magnificent birds left. These would soon depart North Dakota and wing eastward to winter along the Atlantic coast. One hundred thousand were destined for Chesapeake Bay alone.

Later still in the afternoon, with dusk hurrying, we observed a hillside covered with feeding sandhill cranes. How many? I can't guess. Thousands.

"Leo," I asked, "Do snow geese ever mingle with cranes?"

"Hell no. Why?"

"There are four white birds out there, in the middle of the cranes. They have black wing-tips."

"Where?" Leo and Ron asked together.

I pointed and their binoculars scanned the hill. The birds were nervous because we were so near. A gray, squawking cloud lifted and fanned the prairie air. There was a swirl of wings and dust and wonderful noise.

"Oh, would you look at that. Boys, do you know what you just saw? Those were whoopers!" Leo exclaimed. Like a child, almost trembling, he added, "We just spotted four of the world's 144 whooping cranes. In all my years, I've never seen one."

Whooping cranes. Only a gross of them left in the wild. Each year their protected population increases by only a few individuals after surviving a close call with extinction. The whoopers, sandhills, Ron, Leo, and I came together in the only spot where this was possible on the whole of the planet. A prairie miracle. And a brush with extinction.

That's what wandering on the North Dakota prairie in October is like.

Just north of Medina, there is a farm that looks like a Norman Rockwell painting. Here are tall silos the color of the sky. Acres of trees stretch along the road that leads to the property, a barn, and a long driveway leading to two white houses. The houses were placed near the crest of a knoll, overlooking the westward rolling prairie. In the front yard, below the hill and near the road, is a slough. This farmer, whoever he was, was doing well and had still found room for a pesky pothole or two. I could guess that I was going to like this guy.

Ron had wanted me to see this place. We parked and walked up to the front door of the first house. Ron knocked, but nobody answered. We strolled back to the truck and chatted, waiting for someone to arrive. While we talked, I let Rascal out. She made a beeline for the slough.

The dog ran through the cattails. The tops whipped and threw clouds of downy seeds, bursting from their velvet brown casings, to the wind. Then we heard a startling, loud cackle. A bronze, emerald, and jade pheasant rooster blew from the cover, its long tail streaming behind. Rascal leaped into the air to see over the cattails—and, if I knew her, to try to grab the gaudy bird. Then a pheasant hen flushed at her feet, startling her. Now I knew for sure that this was a special place.

We waited in the shadowless light of the cool October dusk. No one came. Ron needed to leave, and so we drove back to my camper and parted. Before he left, I thanked him for the optimism transfusion. "Wait till you talk to the fellow that owns that farm," he grinned out the truck window.

The next morning I shot a few wigeon and gadwalls that came to the frosty pothole, kamikazes to the decoys. Rascal retrieved through quarter-inch ice, diving down three times to get one duck until she caught up to it underwater, applause from the duck blind when she surfaced, duck in mouth. That afternoon I looked for the four stark whooping cranes amid the moving sea of sandhills. I didn't find them, but I got excited when I spotted a small flock of big white birds spinning on an updraft. They were pelicans—in North Dakota! Eighty-five hundred of them nest near Chase Lake. I also saw four birds diving fast: a rare peregrine falcon driving three ducks to water. The ducks were underwater in a flash, the falcon's talons gripping only air as it missed its chance at a meal.

I returned to the Rockwellian farm after supper, and finally met the owner. Ray Heupel is tall, dark-haired, and maybe in his fifties. He wears coveralls and cowboy boots and speaks slowly and thoughtfully. He gripped my hand in a sincere handshake.

Ray farms the Lazy H Ranch with his wife, Mary, and his son, Joseph. Ray always calls him Joseph. Not Joe. His three grown daughters have left, although one is a dairy farmer who lives nearby. The Lazy H and the other lands they manage for absentee owners sprawl for miles, fifty-six hundred rolling acres of cattle and grain. Four generations of the family have lived here since 1899.

When I arrived, Ray and Joseph were fixing a grain auger out near the silos. A farm dog lay in wait for the inevitable escaping mice. The smell of success, the sweet smell of grain fermenting in the tall silos, was in the air. The two men were a good team. Each worked thoroughly, carefully, and competently. I lent a hand where I could, thinking that this was a good life, a nice way to make a living.

Later, Ray and I talked seriously. I had to know more about him and the land because the fate of the prairie's wildlife was in the farmer's hands. Farmers complained that in order to keep the farm, wildlife had to go. But something was different here. The Lazy H was a success. Families had been raised here. Land had been passed down for generations. And still there was room for wildlife. How was that possible? I asked Ray to take me back, back to the good old days.

"When my mom was a little girl, many of the people here depended on the wildlife. Without it, some of them would have starved to death. When my grandparents came in 1899, they had nothing and had to scratch off the land. My grandfather was an avid hunter, you know. Loved it.

"When I was in high school, the grouse here were still so plentiful that it was unreal. That has changed considerably. Farming has changed. But you have to leave some habitat. We don't drain anything on our land, and we don't burn the animals out, either."

A debt had been incurred. The wildlife had nurtured the family. The family would nurture the wildlife. On the Lazy H there are potholes: untouched, restored, and even created. Food plots are left out for the birds. Nesting structures made of flax bales, like perfectly round islands, grace the potholes. And when grain is harvested, the combine leaves a swath or two uncut. A few bucks less for the farmer; food and cover for the wildlife.

"We've done this for years, on our own. Ron's program pays us a little now, and that helps. But we'd do it anyway.

"One incentive is paying us three dollars an acre to leave the wheat stubble on the land after harvest. It gives the geese something to graze on, but more importantly it helps to keep the soil in place and traps the snow where it should be. As far as I'm concerned, it's like finding money. The program is limited to one hundred acres, but that's three hundred dollars. You can buy your wife a pretty nice Christmas present for three hundred dollars. But there are a lot of guys that would normally turn that land over, chisel plow it. Maybe these incentives will get them to think twice."

So why, Ray, why do you do it?

"Whether I get paid or not, I'm going to make room for wildlife. I love wildlife. And after I'm gone, I'll leave something for the future. Maybe my grandchildren will want to hunt. Or just see the wildlife. If I can make a difference, then I'm going to do it. And the land will be healthier, too, you know. That's important.

"You know, you get to the coffee shop and you hear this guy and that guy saying 'Gee-whiz, I had to drill another new well this year, even deeper.' This is what's happening in this country. And I say to them, 'Do you know what has happened? You're not that dumb. Here all these years Uncle Sam has been paying us to drain all these potholes. And where's the water? It's all down in the Gulf of Mexico. We leave nothing to regenerate; it's all gone. If we plug up these drains and fill the potholes with water, we'll have plenty of water in our wells.' But a lot of these guys just hadn't thought of it that way until now. You can't run all the water out of the country.

"Listen, a lot of these guys are paying attention. I think these programs are going to fly. I really do. They see my land and that of some of my neighbors who are doing the same as I am. And they ask us how to get in on this.

"I think this Chase Lake Project will keep going, all the way up the Coteau. It'll be really sad if it doesn't."

Amen, Ray. Amen.

Time to leave. Time to head home for a while, back to Minnesota to see the trees and water and feel damp air on my skin. Time to see Mary Jo. Almost a month had passed since I left home. My mind was a whirl of problems, facts, people, sights, and sounds. With the sun at our backs, Rascal and I spun the rubber eastward.

The heat of summer, unwelcome in October, had returned to parch the already dry soil even more. The canvasbacks had disappeared overnight. The blue-winged teal were probably already skimming the Louisiana coastal marshes. And the mallards and gadwalls would stick around until it grew cold; they would hardly miss me for a while. A painful urge to go home came, suddenly, like a fit. I threw everything into the truck, pointed it east, and left the prairie.

Leaving, I passed the Lazy H. There was no question in my mind that the Chase Lake Project, Ron Stromstad's work, and the caring of men like Ray Heupel and Levi Patzner were the only real hope for the ducks and all other prairie wildlife.

Although the North Dakota prairie will never return completely to its native lushness, with careful management the majority of species will survive. Incentives, education, and heart-to-heart chats over coffee and sweet rolls will help to accomplish the goal.

Who would have ever guessed that the tools most important to the salvation of ducks would be caramel, coffee, and conversation?

Similar steps are also being taken in Canada, most notably in the Quill Lakes region by Ross Melinchuk and his crew, but there is still an air of resistance there. There is no doubt that on the North Dakota prairie the balance is shifting, the chances for success more immediate. Perhaps we are more responsive because we have already extirpated some species, drained the majority of our wetlands, and seen the topsoil blowing for more years. From the bottom, if you are going to go anywhere, it can only be up.

WISCONSIN

Winter plays tag with autumn; the winner is always the same. The ducks, the dog, and I race before its icy breath.

Here is the scene: northwest Wisconsin in the fourth week of October. The only leaves on the trees are those of the tough little scrub oaks, rasping brown in the wind. The sky is sullen, charcoal. Temperature in the twenties. The wind whips from the northwest, blowing across a butterscotch tamarack bog.

Rascal and I are hunkered behind a hump of grass and sand and fallen trees, near the water's edge. In front of us is a bunch of bobbing bluebill decoys, a few mallard fakes, and a bent yellow swath of wild rice. The lake is the color of lead. Flecks of white foam blow from the thin, crested waves. On a hill on the other side of the lake, beneath the oaks and pines, is a friend's snug brown cabin, where Rascal and I spend our nights before the fireplace. Wood smoke climbs its chimney and is torn by the wind.

Although I wear layers and layers of waterfowling clothes, I am very nearly frozen. My knees ache and my nose is a leaky faucet. My ears are red and brittle; if you tweaked one it surely would snap off. To try to keep them warm, I alternately jam my hands into my armpits, blow on them, encase them in cumbersome gloves, wrap them around a steaming coffee cup, or bury them deep in the black dog's fur.

And you know what? I love this. I would rather face the wrath of winter than be caressed by summer's silken hand. This is the price I must pay to see ducks on the wing. There is pleasure in tossing decoys from a boat in a dark world where everyone is asleep but you and your dog, pleasure in moving the decoys around until, in the graying dawn, you are satisfied that they will fool the ducks.

When I began this trip, I had planned to follow the ducks through both Dakotas and down the Missouri, with a side trip into Nebraska. The lingering Dakota prairie summer changed those plans. The ducks had simply ceased their migration, only the silver canvasbacks departing in response to the alarms of their secret clocks. The other ducks were content to bask in the sun and eat grain. I had decided to take advantage of the temporary halt in the migration to make a quick trip home.

On the way home through Minnesota, while stopping to walk the dog, I had scanned a broad blue lake and spotted a raft of bluebills, bobbing black and white far out in the middle of the water. These are the ducks that signify the beginning of winter. No matter how summer hung on in North

Dakota, the sloughs I had visited in Manitoba must have frozen. The migration now would quicken its pace.

I opted to head south into some of my favorite duck country in northwest Wisconsin, a region that is somewhat similar to the parklands of Manitoba and Saskatchewan and certainly was the place that the Turtle Mountain woodlands had reminded me of most. Coming here would also allow me to sneak home to see my wife, only an hour away, and still let me keep track of the ducks.

Lead Poisoning

Before lead shot was banned for waterfowl hunting in the United States in 1990, up to three million waterfowl may have died each year.

Waterfowl may ingest spent lead shot when feeding on heavily hunted marshes or fields. Depending on factors such as the food type, the bird's health, and environmental conditions, the ingestion of as few as one or two lead pellets can result in lead poisoning and death of the bird.

Lead poisoning acts slowly. Digestive juices reduce the shot to lead salts, which enter major body organs through the bloodstream. Affected birds carry their wings in a roofed shape over their backs in the early stages of lead poisoning. As the condition worsens, the bird experiences a green discharge at the anus, digestive tract paralysis, loss of flight, and eventual death due to weakness, predation, or exposure.

Bald eagles that feed on crippled ducks can ingest the shot found in the ducks' tissues. They will succumb to lead poisoning as well.

Because nontoxic steel shot is now mandated by law and the lead shot already in the marshes is being covered by siltation, lead poisoning in waterfowl has been nearly eliminated in the United States. Canada still allows the use of lead shot.

One other factor had urged me to follow the ducks this far east: the attitude of a man from Illinois. Dressing in brand-new camouflage clothes and driving a big, plush Suburban full of the latest waterfowling toys, he had stopped to chat with me while I was in Saskatchewan. He typified money trying to compensate for skill, looking for an easy place to hunt so he won't have to waddle his fat ass too far or work up a sweat. Aldo Leopold had once said that the value of outdoor recreation is in proportion to the degree in which it differs from and contrasts with our everyday life. Hunters (and campers and fishermen) cheat themselves and alienate the nonsporting public when they insist on hauling gadgets and sophisticated motorized equipment into the wild and demand easy access for their pursuits, which serves to dilute the experience and carve up wild areas.

This man also expressed something that I have heard from other hunters: disbelief in the duck crisis.

"Just a plot," he had said. "They've shortened the season and lowered the limit so the guys down south can shoot them all. Well, I'm going to get mine. Hell, the ducks have just moved east, that's all. There ain't no shortage of birds."

He said this while standing in the midst of a veritable desert, the dried, embalmed heart of the world's richest duck production region.

I had to check out the man's theory, not that I believed for a moment that it would be true. This area, one of my favorites, is truly an important part of the Mississippi flyway. The great flocks funnel from the north by following watercourses or hopscotching from lake to lake. They briefly visit the lake country that surrounds the great river's headwaters and tributaries, like the nearby clear St. Croix. A large proportion of birds follows the mother river south; others veer east to their Atlantic coast winter retreats.

It had snowed during the night. The new snow clung to each tree branch, so the Wisconsin woodlands were a tracery of black and white. Cattails bowed their brown heads under the white weight, and deer tracks punctuated the shore.

Unlike the past two mornings, when the sun had risen in a cold blue sky, this dawn had broken in shades of gray: black to slate to iron. You can smell the cold on a day like this. When the October snow comes racing on the breath of arctic gusts, the world becomes so somber that warmth and life beg heed. I cherish this experience. The ducks are so lively in contrast to a world grinding to a white halt. In their winged wanderings there is magic and great urgency. I feel the urgency as a pang of grief, for when the ducks have gone, it will be a very long time before the world breathes again.

I come here the third or fourth week of each October. A tryst. I come to meet the ringbills. Swift, darting little wanderers from the far north, coming from regions untouched by man, breeding on the great, wide deltas of the Athabasca River or the parkland and boreal marshes, setting up housekeeping on mats of floating sedge. Minnesota, Wisconsin, and Michigan, too, are home to smaller breeding populations of ringbills (officially known as ring-necked ducks), but the birds I see and hunt on the eve of winter have come a great distance.

Of all the diving ducks I have often thought that the ringbill is most like the dabblers. One distinguishing feature between these two types of ducks is how they feed. Dabblers merely tip up, butts in the air, and feed in shallow water at neck's reach. Diving ducks do just that, dive, often quite deeply, to feed on wild celery, seeds of pondweeds, and even snails and clams ten to forty feet beneath the surface. I'd like to be underwater to see them fly through that element. My little ringbills, however, when passing through Minnesota and Wisconsin, dine in shallow water on fallen seeds of wild rice. Into the broad yellow stands of this wild grain, ringbills fall from the sky as if they were poured from a bucket. They bob and feed with quiet chuckles.

Ducks can be used as indicators of the earth's health. If the prairie duck's situation epitomizes the crisis on the western plains, the swift ringbill may be used to measure the health of the boreal forest's wetlands.

According to Barry Verbewski, waterfowl biologist for the Province of Manitoba, the nesting area of the ringbill was safe, but he added, with a sad shake of his head: "If we figure out a way to drain those areas," indicating the sedge meadows to the north, "we're all in trouble. We'll have gone too far."

Now, as I scanned the wintery sky for the handsome black-and-white drakes with their glossy black peaked heads, I hoped that their home was safe and that they would—forever—make the long migration to their wintering grounds in Louisiana or Florida.

Rascal, who had been curled in a tight ball, nose under her tail like an Eskimo's husky, jumped to attention next to me. I strained my frozen ears and then heard the faint, quick *whew-whew-whew* of wings. Across the lake, like beads on a string, a train of twenty or more ringbills fought the breeze, silhouettes against the billowy dun sky. Snow like grains of cold sand slanted from the west to beat in tiny taps against my stiff parka and clatter on the dry oak leaves. I gave the ducks a growly *bbrrrt, bbrrrt* on the call and grabbed the icy shotgun. Two sets of eyes followed the birds.

All of a sudden, from a height of sixty or seventy yards, the ringbills tumbled down on cupped wings, squeezing the air beneath them so that it gasped as it ripped through their primaries. Like feathered stones they dropped to the decoys. Rascal watched. I creaked to my feet. The shotgun wavered in front of me, steadied, threw hot steel through the sky. Fruits of the far north fell, lay white-breasted ripe on the water, waiting for Rascal.

On command she forged through steel gray ice water, snatched the ringbill, and turned toward the duck blind. Rascal and I shivered in unison. I hefted the handsome bird she had retrieved, smoothed its ruffled feathers, thought of the far place whence it came: the sedge, the rivers, the short summer. I felt its plump breast, fattened with the golden Minnesota wild rice. There is far more to duck hunting than merely killing birds.

From the north came the tootling of tundra swans. Like white jumbo aircraft they sailed by. Soon the last of the ducks would come through, and for a while a few would hang on at this Burnett County lake, watching the ice grow out from shore. And when only the giant swans were left, standing near an open hole in the middle, winter would come to stay. Then the swans too would drift away.

That would be soon, only days, at most, weeks. Rascal and I needed to be about our business.

NEBRASKA

Five billion birds migrate north to south, then south to north, across the North American continent. Make that five billion and four migrants, including Rascal and me, and Ernie and Marlene.

Ernie and Marlene are just two of the most recent additions to the autumn migration. As I fight a headwind on Interstate 90 in southern Minnesota, driving through snow so dense that my vision is limited to only yards, Ernie and Marlene pass me, their pick-up truck towing a monster of a travel trailer. They wave, a nice retired couple.

I know their names because they painted them in script on the back of their trailer. No doubt they are migrating to the Southwest to spend the winter. Snowbirds. When they pass, I quickly pull up almost to their bumper to let them break the thirty-mile-per-hour headwind. You can almost hear my truck sigh in relief.

It is November now. I had paused at home, once I left Wisconsin, to see my patient wife and to sneak into the stark forest to hunt deer. Fortunately, a fat eight-point buck appeared the first day. He had, like a dog, sniffed his way down a trail past my stand, through the barren aspens, hormones stirred by the scent of a doe in heat. When his heart stopped, mine beat ferociously and my hands shook. Once home, in a flurry of flashing knives, Mary Jo and I butchered the deer, our winter meat, and then I hastily departed.

Perhaps I had waited too long. Winter had come to Minnesota. Rascal snoozed while I drove blindly, the long miles white with boredom. Ernie and Marlene made good time west and I stayed on their tail until they stopped for lunch. I pressed on, fighting the wind.

You can drive an amazingly long time with a Thermos full of coffee and a supply of sandwiches and cookies readily at hand. But because of the terrible wind and swirling snow, eleven hours on the road had brought us only to little Murdo, South Dakota, where we turned south, in the dark.

On Highway 83 we crossed the deep, dusky valley of the White River as it wound its way east to the muddy Missouri. There was no traffic in either direction, and there were very few lights beside the road to indicate human habitation. Tired and on a lonely highway, I pressed on for no particular reason except that I wanted to reach Nebraska. At least the wind and snow were behind us.

Going over a hill I had to swerve to the left, piling on the brakes. Unexpectedly, a man in soiled trousers, walking a crooked walk, stood in the southbound lane. I will never forget his face in the glare of my head-lights: a tortured map of scowling seams creased into his face by permanent hate and despair so profound I could feel them. He lifted a fist to me as I swerved around him. He did not know me, and he hated me nonetheless. Never had I felt anything like that. Obviously the man was exceedingly, emphatically, decidedly drunk.

Startled, I looked around. A small village had sprung up in the dark: row upon row of identical little houses, each with a single yard lamp. An Indian reservation. An outpost of despair.

Now I understood the man, for I had seen his brothers all through my trip. They were a people lost between worlds: unable to adapt to the white man's, unable to keep hold of their own.

There is little question that what the European settlers did to the American Indians ranks as one of the greatest atrocities of man. The white culture destroyed the Indian. It could not abide a rival culture, especially one that did not exploit natural resources.

It was easy to understand the weaving drunk's hate. Were the wild creatures who have been similarly displaced capable of it, they would no doubt show their wrath, as well.

The sun rose clear and yellow over the Nebraska prairie, casting its bright light on the hissing waters of the twenty-eight hundred-acre Merritt Reservoir. A steady, cool wind blew from the west, and small waves rolled up on the sandy shore. Rascal was romping outside in the dewy grass, while I stood in the little camper, so comfortable now as my home, frying bacon and eggs and making toast over a flame.

Watching out the window, I saw Rascal come to a slow creep, face to the wind, nose up. She looked around for me. Her tail began to work frantically, round and round, and then she burst forward. A blur of cackling white birds erupted from the grass. Sharp-tailed grouse. She bounced forward like a dog on a pogo stick, pounding the late risers into the air. Then she turned and ran back to the camper.

"For heaven's sake," she stared through the camper screen door, "get your butt out here. There are grouse all over the place." Then, mumbling to herself as she wagged back to where the grouse had been, "Where's the boss when you need him, anyway?"

We had crept through to the little town of Valentine in a road-weary daze. Everyone in town had gone to bed; there was not one vehicle or person on the village streets. Then we had driven the twenty-six miles farther to this reservoir.

Even in the dark I could see that this prairie was different from those farther north, that the Nebraska sandhills would be something special. Agriculture was far rarer. Barbed-wire fences told us that this was ranch country. Also, clumps of cedar grew here and there, especially on the abrupt, carven hillsides. When we crossed the Snake River, which flows from the reservoir, we stopped to smell and listen. I was startled to hear rapids, and even in the darkness I could see the river's ripping whitewater.

Now we had been in the Sandhills for two full days, and wonderful country it is. Ranches run thirty thousand acres or more in size. Can't cross them in a day on horseback, as the old saying goes. On hillsides, cowboys sit astride dark horses; if you have a good imagination, you can see them smoking roll-your-owns. Though heavily grazed, the land still hosts many of the plant species, and some of the wildlife, of the true tall-grass prairie. The Sandhills seem more arid and yet more well watered than the Dakota and Canadian prairies. The sand that can run as deep as 180 feet makes the prairie seem parched. Yet the vast Ogallala aquifer on top of which it sits provides clear, fast streams. In addition, hundreds of small lakes lie in depressions lower than the water table and give the appearance of watery abundance.

It is this water that attracts the ducks. Though these wetlands share some characteristics with the potholes farther north, they can't truly be called by the same name. Whereas the potholes are the fluid remains of glaciers, replenished by rain and snow, the Sandhill wetlands were formed by an entirely different process.

Long ago, the dwindling waters of an ancient sea, probably located in present-day Wyoming, exposed its sandy bed. What must have been cataclysmic winds stirred that seabed and with a force that now can only be imagined picked up billions of tons of sand and deposited them in north central Nebraska. The wind continued to shape the hills into what look very much like huge sand dunes.

Over time, the prairie grasses took root. Sand-love grass, big and little bluestem, prairie sand-reed, and Indian grass covered the hills and meadows. Spiky yucca plants grew, as did wild sunflowers and the many showy forbs that helped to lock the shifting sands into place.

In the low places the Sandhill lakes formed, large and small, number-
ing in the thousands. Spring rains raised the water table, flooding additional
lowlands. With such natural underground irrigation, the deep, dense root
mats of the grasses found drinking easy, and along rivers and lakes, cottonwood, willow, elm, ash, and hackberry trees made homes. In time, bur oak,
red cedar, and juniper trees found their niches on the uplands, checked by
fire and countless bison from foresting the prairie. In drier parcels, even a
few desert plants, such as little sandspurs and the white-spiked yuccas,
grow.

The world here is dominated by sky and rolling plains. It is over those
plains, in that clear sky, that the ducks and geese and myriad other birds
of the Central Flyway pass. Cattle, not grain, replaced the bison on this
prairie, and although overgrazing has led to some deterioration of the
landscape, the land has not been subjected to the widespread alteration
found on the more northern prairies. What agriculture there is on these
sandy plains is found beneath the rolling pivot irrigation systems that scribe
a circular path as the overhead watering system revolves around its axis.
Whereas the native grass had deep roots that could tap the groundwater,
corn does not and so water is pumped up and sprayed down, and mixed
with the excessive amount of fertilizers needed on this sandy soil. The
irrigation results in both lowering the water table (which in turn causes
some wetlands to become dry) and polluting it with nitrates. In recent years
there seems to be a decline in such irrigation practices.

Although ducks do breed here in comparatively large numbers (mallards, blue-winged teal, and gadwalls are the most common; pintails, red-
heads, ruddy ducks, and shovelers are also found), the role of the Sandhill
wetlands, and indeed of all wetlands throughout Nebraska, is primarily as
migration habitat.

The four flyways of North America are really more a political tool for
waterfowl management than a geographical reality. The Central Flyway,
however, comes the nearest to being an accurate depiction of duck migration, for the birds that use it fly almost due south. Nebraska, with the
Sandhills and other well-watered regions, thus provides an important resting place during spring and fall migrations.

Nearby Valentine National Wildlife Refuge, seventy-two thousand
acres of rolling prairie and sparkling lakes, was established in 1935 to
protect waterfowl habitat. It is not uncommon during May or October to
see 150,000 ducks gathered on the refuge alone. There are many other

wetlands, in private ownership and in varying degrees of health, scattered throughout the hills. Some 260 species of birds pass through, and herons, terns, shorebirds, pelicans, and songbirds nest here.

Although the predators that hamper waterfowl production farther north also exist here, the bull snake most likely contributes most to the loss of eggs. Slithering under the nesting hen, up to six feet of dark-blotched snake gulps the eggs right out from beneath her.

I fell in love with the Sandhills. The ridges roll on and on, and when the sun sets orange and the sky grows purple you can feel here, as probably nowhere else on the prairie, that you have stepped back in time. Human impact is still at a minimum. Few lights shine at night. You see deer feeding with cattle. You see ducks fly into the lakes.

Bordering on arid yet with a wealth of groundwater, the Sandhills not only are critical waterfowl habitat but also are one of the most unusual places to view ducks that I have been. I could not shake the feeling of surprise every time I stumbled across a little lake and its attendant birds. Ducks in a desert.

I was lowering the camper when Rascal came back. She had gone to see if any more grouse were to be found and, disappointed, looked to me to see if anything good might happen.

I had decided not to hunt ducks here, for no particular reason except that I had no desire to do so and was content to merely watch them. But that doesn't mean I had no desire to hunt at all. The Sandhills offered a unique opportunity to hunt prairie grouse.

Driving on the prairie trails here is treacherous. The sand is as fine as sugar, and I'm quite sure that it would be possible to spin your way right down to the netherworld and have the sand cover you up. Swallowed by prairie. I put the truck in four-wheel drive and lumbered like a turtle with my home on my back up and down the steep trails.

Len McDaniel, the Valentine refuge manager (who does spring waterfowl nesting-pair counts on horseback—imagine), told me to walk with the wind while hunting sharptail. Normally when working a dog you try to hunt into the wind to aid scenting. But this crusty westerner knows prairie grouse better than most. (When I had stopped at headquarters and asked for Mr. McDaniel, a lean, bearded man said in a distinctive cowboy twang, "Whadya want to see that ornery sombitch for?"—it was McDaniel himself.)

"You cain't work into the wind. You hafta walk ta other way. See, the sharptail sit just over the top of the hills, protected, letting the wind warsh over them. If you walk upwind, they'll spot you comin'."

Rascal and I followed his instruction. A long, low hill, green clumps of yucca, tan grass, and the occasional thicket of ashen buckbrush spread before us to the edge of the earth. Reluctant to walk with the wind, Rascal kept turning around and required encouragement. Slowly we climbed, reaching the top together.

Walking the Sandhills is exhausting. The sandy soil gives beneath your feet, and the dry air stings your lips. The grass clutches at your boots. Sandspurs, the size of silver dollars and with long, sharp spines, painfully grab a dog's paws. And though the prairie elsewhere is flat, here it rolls like the storm-tossed Atlantic.

Rascal quickly became birdy. Small dinner-plate depressions, where the grouse had been resting and dusting themselves, littered the sandy soil. She moved quickly, thoroughly sniffing them. I watched her spinning tail. I took a step forward.

Feathered bombs exploded. Mostly white birds launched in a confusion of whirring wings and cackling, splattering the earth beneath them with droppings. I swung the shotgun and sent a charge toward a departing bird. A clean miss. The second bird I pulled on wasn't quite so lucky and met the pellets somewhere in the Nebraska sky, a slow shower of feathers raining down, the bird thumping heavily into the grass. Rascal ran to retrieve. Yep, they'd been just over the top of the hill with the wind "warshing" over them.

Gayly, the black dog brought the prairie grouse to me, and I admired its speckled coat and white-stockinged legs. I carefully slid the bird into my game vest, thinking of the purple flesh that would be a meal.

We walked off toward the next long hill, maybe a half mile distant, over which the remaining eight or ten grouse had flown in their typical sharptail flap-and-glide, flap-and-glide. An endless blue dome spanned our world, white tufted clouds skittering on the breeze. Rascal startled a kangaroo rat gathering seeds. The long, tufted tail whipped as the big-eyed rodent shot down its burrow. To our left, a marsh that had been hidden from view peeked into sight. Cottonwoods rimmed the north side, and while we

watched, two dozen mallards set their wings and lazed their way gently
down to the water.

Leaving the Sandhills wasn't going to be easy.

A week in Nebraska already, and November marches on. The western
half of Nebraska has a few roads north of the interstate. Damn fine. Rascal
and I wandered west and hunted the big Canada geese on the North Platte
River (barely ankle deep, a block wide, and so fast it'll knock you off your
feet) near the little town of Broadwater. In the morning, as the eastern sky
turned rose over the shadowy hills, the geese would begin talking, sitting on
their sandbar roosts in the dancing river.

I hunted here with Tom Rosdail, a quiet, amicable Iowa transplant.
He works for Cabela's, the mail-order supplier of outdoor gear in nearby
Sydney. We hunted on the company's private land, a rolling spread and
former farm on the banks of the North Platte, complete with deluxe goose
pits, man-made potholes, and huge spreads of decoys scattered about.

We drove up from Sydney in the dark, Rascal and Tom's chocolate
Lab, Bosco, jittery in the back of Tom's Land Cruiser. We strolled to the
blind, slid back the hatch covers, and climbed inside. Rascal stayed outside
(Bosco, rightfully, considered the pit her turf and wouldn't tolerate my dog
inside—in fact, ripped Rascal's face with a slash of fangs the instant they
first met), and I covered her with straw to hide her while Bosco sat inside by
her boss.

The day dawned, and the ducks flew in great numbers, thousands in a
swirling cloud, part of the ten thousand mallards that spend the winter
here. Then the geese warmed up, and maybe some cranes, and the entire
world was filled with goose talk and mallard squabbling.

Occasionally, a few geese strayed near. We tried to seduce them with
our goose calls as we peered up through the head holes in the sliding pit
covers, our heads shielded from above by inverted, straw-thatched wicker
baskets mounted on wire legs. We stuck our heads through the outhouse-
like holes and watched for geese through the gap. Based on our experience,
though, no one need worry about Canada geese becoming extinct because
of hunting pressure. We shot only a few in the two days, Rascal and Bosco
each making beautiful retrieves on the ten-pound birds.

The best part of the experience was breakfast in the pit. Yup. During a
slow spell, Tom would begin to fry up eggs and moose steaks and pour

coffee and orange juice, cooking on the propane stove inside the ten-by-five-foot pit. Then we'd slide the hatches back, put our steaming breakfasts on the pit's edge, and eat happily while the cool wind blew and cranes crooned overhead. The two dogs watched us boldly.

As you travel east on Interstate 80, parallel to the great Platte River, you get a sense of a world out of whack, of priorities gone astray. Sandhill cranes are a fixture here, and have been for at least the last ten million years. At no other place in the entire world is there a larger gathering of cranes of any type than in March along the Platte, when five hundred thousand of the great gray birds rest and feed after flying, nonstop, the six hundred miles from their wintering grounds.

Once the Platte and North Platte were broad, shallow rivers, scoured yearly by the spring snowmelt rushing from Colorado and Wyoming. Where the channel was two thousand feet wide and only six inches deep, four-fifths of the world's sandhill cranes would descend for a month or more to roost in the vegetation-free river and feed in nearby meadows.

Then the river changed. Man saw the water as a way to irrigate his fields and power his factories. Seventy percent of the water was claimed by man, narrowing places in the river by ninety percent. Trees grew in the river where only sandbars once could exist. Water tables dropped, and agriculture moved in to the river's edge, destroying the meadows.

Each year the cranes returned, for their faith is eternal, even molecular, and found fewer and fewer places where they could roost safe from predators. And each year man took more water, so that city people could water their lawns, wash their cars, have green golf courses.

Now, the world's most impressive crane population is forced to crowd into the small stretch of water that remains, unable to go elsewhere because no place else exists that meets their needs.

Never mind that the cranes' claim to the river and its water pre dates ours by 9,999,900 years.

Near York, in eastern Nebraska, a male northern harrier sailed low over a marsh on long, narrow wings, its gray back shining in the sun. As we watched, a pheasant hen, nervous, dashed from the thin grass toward shelter. The hawk swooped, too late, climbed, and continued on. The pheasant was safe.

"Would you look at that," my companion said, interrupting his lunch.

All along my journey I had had the pleasure of meeting dedicated wildlife professionals who would take the time to show me around and try to explain the local status of waterfowl and wildlife. For me, the discussions added to a holistic view of migration and the story of waterfowl. For those with whom I spoke, the discussions provided a chance to share their sense of urgency to stop the dismal trend of habitat destruction, loss of wildlife, and general degradation of the environment. Some wanted to share their hope and enthusiasm; others expressed only doom. I had noticed that the older the person, the less hope he held for waterfowl. Younger managers believed that if we acted quickly, waterfowl and wetlands would survive—maybe even flourish.

Dick Gersib was a young, enthusiastic, and hopeful wetlands specialist for the Nebraska Game and Parks Commission. As he showed me around the rainwater basins of south central Nebraska, he explained that the basins are both critical to waterfowl and critically ill. Shallow, incredibly fertile, and stretching below an arch in the thirty-five-degree isotherm that the birds follow north, these broad wetlands open early, attract millions of waterfowl from the three westernmost flyways, and are of great importance not only to waterfowl survival, but also to their breeding success once they reach the north.

We were eating our lunch in a government car while we watched ducks trade in and out of the basin when Dick began to talk:

"You really can't get a perspective on how important these basins are to breeding birds without realizing how critical body weight and fat are to their reproduction and survival. No, they don't lay their eggs here, but the basins provide that crucial body weight.

"In spring, the birds have to pick up body fat. A lot of the birds leave for the breeding grounds in poor shape. Obviously, between the wintering and breeding grounds they have to pick up a lot of their energy reserves someplace. That someplace is here."

My pencil was smoking.

"You're looking at a four-hundred-acre basin. In the spring this one basin will consistently hold nearly one hundred thousand birds, and our research shows that they are feeding nearly all the time. Also, the basins provide a secondary pairing area for those birds, especially pintails, that haven't yet selected a mate.

"Fifty percent of the continental breeding population of mallards use the rainwater basins in spring. So do 30 percent of all pintails. In one aerial count, we documented that 90 percent of the continent's white-fronted geese were here at the same time!"

I looked out over the canary grass, down the gradual incline that formed the basin, and beyond the reddish smartweed that lay low and vinelike before the water began, trying to imagine the spectacle of millions of ducks and millions of geese, all feeding here at once, waiting for winter to leave the north. We watched through binoculars as ducks got up, stretched their wings in short, circling flights, and disappeared again into the heavily vegetated marsh. Sleek pintails, the first real concentration of the species I'd seen so far, were the most numerous. Mallards and teals traded back and forth. Coots looked like lumps of mud sitting in the basin.

We finished our lunch, then drove on slowly down the gridwork of country roads. Gravel clattered on the undercarriage.

We stopped next to a trench, a long, perfectly straight, rigidly rectangular pit full of water and little else. No ducks.

"You want to see rape and pillage?" Dick said, resigned anger in his voice. "Look what has been done to the basins. We've lost 90 percent of them, and those that are left are usually severely degraded. What the farmers couldn't drain, they put into a concentration pit, like this one.

"The really tough part is that those pits were all cost-shared by the government. We paid for this destruction, you and I, every time we wrote a check to the IRS. Now, if there's any hope of restoring them, we'll have to pay the landowners again.

"Here's my sales pitch. The money we put into a relatively few acres here will benefit millions of waterfowl across the prairie-pothole region, all the way to Alaska and the arctic. Not only that, there are also benefits to society in general, such as flood control and better water quality. But we have to sell it.

"We've targeted up to 150 basins for work. That'll take money. And it shouldn't be the landowners' responsibility to pay for this; it should be society as a whole. It sure shouldn't be the hunters—they've been carrying the load for a long time."

The rainwater basins had just recently become a part of the North American Waterfowl Management Plan, and Dick was excited about the prospect. It had been an uphill battle. Human nature being what it is, many of his counterparts did not agree with spending money on anything but wintering and breeding grounds. But faced with the evidence that these basins provided critical spring staging and feeding habitat, and that as the basins dwindled in number waterfowl were forced to concentrate on the remaining few (resulting in massive avian cholera outbreaks that have killed two hundred thousand waterfowl since 1975), the choice was clear: restore the rainwater basins or face catastrophic losses of waterfowl.

As Dick drove me back to my truck, he told me about one massive basin that had been totally destroyed. Rather than being despondent, he perked up—a strange reaction. As if reading my mind, he turned to me and said, "You have to stay optimistic. If it's the last thing I do, I'll see that basin restored. I think the timing is right for the public to support this. If we don't win the battle this time around, we probably won't have another chance."

Whew! Doesn't that sound familiar?

A rainwater basin is different from a prairie pothole. To really know a basin, you must walk through it. Rascal and I had done just that the day after my travels with Dick Gersib.

I noticed right away that the incline that defines a basin is so slight that you hardly realize you are walking downhill until you feel the soil become claylike and slippery with moisture. The grasses give way to the vines of smartweed tugging at your boots. Eventually, the basin becomes more wet than dry, and you stumble from hummock to hummock, hopelessly trying to avoid getting your feet wet.

The land is farmed up to, or even within, a basin's border. As it was November, the corn was down, and all wildlife had been pushed to the shelter of the basins. No doubt these basins were as important to resident creatures as they were to the migratory ones.

We shot a few pheasants here. I remember one in particular, a wary bird that had led Rascal on a merry chase, the dog pulled by the scent like a toy on a string. It is fascinating to watch a dog interpret the behavior of pheasants. Had I been alone, the bird would have simply held tight or snuck off, leaving me to think the cover devoid of life. But by following Rascal, I saw written on the damp surface of the basin the tracery path of a wise rooster.

Somehow, though, the bird made a mistake and put itself on a small, dry point surrounded by water. Pheasants don't like water. The dog's motions became intense, her snorting rhythmic and deep, her tail a windmill of excitement. I stepped forward with the gun ready and was there when she flushed the bird.

A glory of color and life flew from the smartweed, its long, pointed tail streaming behind. A lone stand of phragmites grew nearby, and the bird struggled on thundering wings to quickly put it between us. As it rounded the edge of the reeds, I fired a hopeful shot.

I did not know if I had hit the bird or not, but I sent the dog anyway. In hunting, there is no crime greater than leaving a crippled animal. Rascal sped off. I heard sloshing, and then she was coming back, around the other side of the reeds, but without the bird. Her head was in the grasses and smartweed, and I knew we had a runner.

You put your faith in your dog at this point. I watched her work intently in a small area, and I was sure she would find the bird quickly. But after minutes of snuffling went by, she began to cast in wide circles. I knew the trail was lost.

I went to the area of the fall and called Rascal to me. The bird must be there someplace. I was feeling sick. I detest losing game.

Rascal searched. We looked for about twenty minutes before, resigned, I began to walk away.

Rascal stopped where we both had looked a dozen times, peering into a dome-shaped hump of bent grass. Her ears went up, her body went rigid. She looked excitedly at me.

"Good girl, Rascal. Fetch it up."

She stuck her head into the hump. The grass moved. Haunches straining, she pulled backward. Out popped her head, and in her mouth was the gorgeous rooster, only wing-tipped and very much alive. She quickly brought the clawing bird to me.

I wrung its neck, something I do not like to do, and, I hope, neither does any hunter. The big bird went limp, and the light in its eyes disappeared. Russet, gold, green, and red, with spurs almost a half inch long. The weight of the bird felt good in my game vest.

We were leaving Nebraska, and I had some fine eating birds to ship home. Kneeling behind the truck for shelter from the frigid, seeking wind, I cleaned our three roosters and wrapped them in plastic. I've found that if I turn the camper refrigerator to "high," I can freeze game in a couple hours. In that time, I'd be near a city and a UPS depot.

Looking at my hands, I saw the blood and it occurred to me that there has been a lot of blood on my hands during my life, the blood of deer and birds and fish of all kinds.

There are people in our society who are offended by all this. Many would like to end my hunting, all hunting. It is cruel, they say. Sick.

I wonder. At least the blood on my hands is visible. Something deep inside me tells me that hunting is necessary. I am a link in the chain of life. I eat to live. Creatures die so that I can eat. Is it not healthier, then, for me to participate in the consequences of my own life? Or should I pay someone else to kill my meat, wrap it in cellophane, and present it on a Styrofoam tray?

Until recently, I had never found it necessary to justify my hunting. Does the wolf? Does the goshawk? Does it make any difference to the deer whether it is killed and eaten by me or by a wolf? Was its life any less meaningful or beautiful? Was there less dignity in its death?

I know what death looks like and what remorse is. I know that participating in the cycle is right and, if done thoughtfully, less harmful to the environment. No fields were cleared, grain raised, herbicides sprayed, or fossil fuels used to grow my meat or the vegetation that fed it.

There are both hawks and vultures in this world. Vultures sit and watch the highways, waiting for some unlucky creature to die, a tasty roadkill. Hawks soar, swoop, catch, and kill their own prey, hear their dinner's death wail.

There is nothing wrong with being a vulture. But I aspire to be a hawk.

ILLINOIS

Despite the fact that they hardly knew me and that I showed up at supper time, and despite the fact that in the middle of the night Rascal climbed three flights of stairs to their bedroom—twice—and scared the dickens out of them, Frank and Esther Bellrose were very nice to me. I had come to Havana, Illinois, generally following the much-abused Illinois River Valley through rolling farm country and past barns that proclaimed "Start Your Day with Pork" to talk with Frank Bellrose.

If ever there were a waterfowl guru, it is Frank. Since 1938 he has devoted his life to waterfowl ecology as principal scientist for the Illinois Natural History Survey. His research has led to a much-improved understanding of waterfowl migration, and he developed and documented the concept of migration corridors, those narrow aerial pathways that define the patterns of travel, many of which flow east and west. Frank, who has written countless technical articles, as well as the definitive *Ducks, Geese and Swans of North America*, may well be considered the world's expert on the wood duck. In fact, he took time from his work on a book on that subject to talk to me.

Winter had followed me to Illinois. I picked it up in Iowa in the form of blowing snow whipped by ferocious northwest winds, and it rode my bumper down the pike to Havana. Eighteen degrees was the low during the night.

After supper, Frank and I sat in the comfortable basement rec room amid books, western art, and depictions of waterfowl of every type. We talked into the night about ducks, their migration, their plight, and their future, while winter leaned into its task outdoors. I was grateful for the warm place and the conversation.

We chatted about the Illinois River and its valley, as well as the changes Frank had seen in his seventy-three years. The beginning of the end for the natural order along the Illinois was the diversion of Lake Michigan water into its headwaters in 1900 to flush the city's human and industrial waste away from the big lake that provides its drinking water. In the following years, dams sprang up and levees were constructed. The result was that the periodically flooding bottomland hardwood forests, which provided vast nesting areas for wood ducks and mast (acorns) for several duck species, were cleared for agriculture. Once the natural flood-and-dry cycle was broken, siltation and pollution from increased agriculture and city waste promoted the growth of aquatic and moist-soil vegetation, which in turn caused the disappearance of two other critical foods: fingernail clams and snails. The habitat became all but useless to the once massive migrations of waterfowl.

What habitat still exists is manipulated, even created, by large hunting clubs and to some degree by the state to mimic, through pumped flooding, the natural cycle and to encourage the growth of such moist-soil duck foods as smartweed. Although this manipulation may at first seem merely to provide a way for hunters to kill more ducks, the end result is that more ducks reach the wintering grounds in better shape than before, and the food they take on during their stay here helps to augment the taxed food sources in the Deep South. So the ducks pay their way.

Even though it may seem ironic to provide habitat at the expense of some ducks' lives, as Frank said, "If you look at the duck clubs' providing all this food, despite their harvest of birds, they are really benefiting the ducks. Without that food source, many of those ducks may have died anyway."

Frank Bellrose was the first researcher to document many facets of duck migration, including the fact that ducks navigate at night by using the stars. After World War II, Frank had the idea of putting radios on ducks to monitor their movements. Informed that the technology just wasn't there and that the radios would have to be so large the birds wouldn't be able to fly, he settled on using little "taillights," simple battery-and-bulb systems connected only by wires.

"We released those birds on cloudy nights and on clear ones. On the overcast nights, the birds wandered rather aimlessly, but on a clear night the birds headed straight north. The obvious conclusion was that they used celestial navigation. We could follow the lights sometimes for two miles. Well, I was excited. It was the first night in my life I couldn't sleep."

Then chuckling, he went on. "There were some farmers sitting on their front porches and they came over to see what was going on. They couldn't figure out what the heck those lights were they saw zipping by their houses!"

The house was quiet. Esther had gone to bed, and Rascal lay napping on the carpet. I watched Frank as he talked, his square-jawed face crowned by a white crew cut, his long fingers quietly working a pencil on a scratch pad. What a mind! What curiosity! Imagine putting taillights on ducks. He continued to talk slowly about his lifelong work with wood ducks and his pioneering of the use of radar to map out the migration corridors. Here was a man who saw the marvels of nature, and for most of his seventy-three years had wondered why, how. Ducks had given him much. He had returned the favor.

A pattern seemed to be forming. Frank's first boss had been one of Aldo Leopold's students, and Frank himself had met the famous conservationist. One can only wonder what the world would be like today if we had adopted Leopold's farsighted philosophy half a century ago. Instead, we now marvel at how dismally true his predictions were. Frank Bellrose was a link in the chain forged by Aldo Leopold; he had taken that philosophy and put it into action.

A yawn split my face, rudely. I was exhausted, but I had one more question: Is there room for optimism about the future of waterfowl?

"What it comes down to is this," Frank said, smiling. "There are things we can do, should do. We've fallen victim to government programs that promote destruction, to that 'Oh, we've got to feed the world' mentality. As long as they guarantee the price of wheat, I doubt that prairie farmers will do anything meaningful to benefit wildlife. Every decline of waterfowl in this century can be traced to conditions on these breeding grounds. This is where we should be spending our money."

He paused, looked up at me.

"All we need is proper land management: places that should be grass, should be left in grass. Government programs can put those lands back into grass and cattle, which would be much better for waterfowl. But even if it does change, how long will that last?"

"What do you mean, Frank?"

"Well, how long will it be before there are so many people that nothing will make a difference? As long as the human population continues to grow unchecked, I'm pessimistic. Human impact on the land is just too great. And when it comes down to it, human needs always come before the needs of wildlife. When ducks and humans compete, the ducks always lose. The problem is sociological, not biological."

I must have looked depressed. As if remembering my hopeful expression when asking this last question, Frank mustered a smile. "Of course we can save part of it, you know. That would be something good, something worth fighting for."

With that, I closed my notebook, turned off the tape recorder, and stood up to stretch. We chatted for a few more minutes about lighter subjects before I took Rascal out into the cold Illinois night for a quick walk. When I returned, the lights were off except in the room in which I was to sleep. I crawled into my sleeping bag on the couch and turned out the lights.

But it was a long time before I fell asleep.

"I feel kind of cheated, you know?"

"How do you mean," I replied.

The young gas-station attendant in hilly, forested Jonesboro, Illinois, thought a moment as he leaned against the camper. We'd been talking about ducks and my trip.

"Well, it's just that my daddy tells me 'bout all the ducks they used to see, and how good the huntin' was, and me and my brother, why, we go just as often as we can, and some days we don't see nothin'. Today, we shot a couple of wood ducks, and, boy, they sure were purty, and we had a good time. But it would be arful nice to just see more ducks."

"She bite?" he asked in a moderately slow southern accent. (Yes, indeedy, the South starts in Illinois.) He hooked his thumb toward Rascal.

"Nope. Probably lick your face off. Go ahead."

He reached into the open truck window. Rascal needed no prompting. Soon she was squirming and licking.

"She gone with you all that way?"

I nodded.

"Man, what a trip! Is it as dry up north as they been sayin'?"

I said it was, maybe even drier.

"You know, we've been takin' it arful easy on them ducks. Even when we can, we don't shoot our limit, some days. Some days we do, cain't hep it. I just wish this drought would end. Maybe then we'd see more ducks. You huntin' 'round here?"

"Nope. Just passin' through. I'm on my way to Arkansas and Louisiana. Going to spend the night by Union County Refuge. Do you know if there's a pay phone there? I'd like to call my wife."

"Don't think there is. You'll see plenty of geese there. Man!" His eyes rolled wide. "You can use my phone, if you got a credit card. Go on in, I'll be 'long shortly."

I thanked him, chuckling to myself. "'Long shortly.'" The play on words struck me as funny.

I went into the warm gas station, glad to get out of the cold December wind. Fine flakes of snow swirled on the breeze outside the window. I made a short, happy call to Mary Jo, paid the man for the gas, and started to leave.

"You really writin' a book about ducks?" he asked as I reached the door.

"Yup. Be out in fall of '91."

"Well, I'll be lookin' for it. Hey, maybe by that time we'll have more ducks!"

Yes, I thought as I waved goodbye, and maybe we'll have even fewer.

––––––––––––––––

It is the beginning of the second week of December. (You may have a hard time accounting for all my days if you're trying to keep track.) Most days I while away the time peering through binoculars along rivers and near marshes, on the lookout for ducks and geese. Occasionally, I've stopped for a day, stayed in a motel, and done laundry. Some days are just long days spent on the road. The United States looks exactly the same everywhere you go, except for the topography, if you travel only on freeways. Golden arches loom, familiar gas-station signs poke skyward on long poles, and chain motels proclaim their low rates on billboards as you wheel wearily along.

Back roads are better but slower. This trip wasn't intended to be a quest for America. Steinbeck and Moon have done that already. This is a quest for waterfowl, and maybe a bit more. You be the judge.

Sometimes traveling is just like taking snapshots. Only bits and pieces come away with you, and you tuck them in the photo album of your mind. Here are some snapshots from my album.

Photo one: A dead opossum on the road. A steep valley to the west. Deep oak forest climbing the hill. The slow Illinois River below, to the left, steel-colored through the timber.

Never saw an opossum before, and this one is lying on its side as if it weren't even hurt, its naked tail curled forward. I must be in the South now.

I swerve to avoid the dead opossum. When I look in the rearview mirror, it is gone. Naw, couldn't be.

Photo two: Snow swirling thickly, already lying two inches thick on the grass. Southern Illinois has ground to a halt. No one drives in such a "blizzard." I laugh at the warnings on the radio. Come to Minnesota in December, I think. It is hard to see where the horizon is, the snow is so thick. Beautiful. I know there are big hills nearby. From somewhere to the east I hear geese coming. Canadas.

Then, as if they had stepped from behind a curtain, they are there, wheeling, black on white. *Gerunk, ger-RUNK*, I squeeze from my throat. They need no urging. The leader cups its wings and parachutes toward the shallow pond near the cornfield. Black legs drop, swing forward, webs spread. One character is an acrobat, tumbles this way and that, one leg down, then the other. Must be a teenager.

Photo three: Horseshoe Bend Refuge. I see my first buttressed cypress trees, holding their skirts up against the rising water. I never expected to see them here, in Illinois. Big gaudy greenheads swim in the dark, watery forest. In and out of the trees. Skirting the skim ice that formed during the night. Strange to see ducks swimming beneath trees.

Stranger still. More geese. They are flying from the north, and when they get overhead, maybe two hundred of them, they turn into the north wind and begin to drop, some sideslipping, others plummeting like feathered bombs. And yes — good God! — they're coming into the cypresses. Falling through the trees! They swoop toward an open area in the middle of the forest, drop in twos and threes, then tens and twenties until it is raining big, black Canada geese, like acorns falling through the trees. *Splat, hiss.* Into the cypress lake.

The mallards continue feeding.

Photo four: Bayou Meto, Arkansas. All across the prairie of eastern Arkansas hawks stood at attention on each and every fencepost, a huge conglomeration of northern harriers, red-tails, broad-wings, and others, making me think of my home near Hawk Ridge, a place where countless hawks (some days you can be dazzled by thousands) funnel through. They are reluctant to cross the broad, blue waters of Lake Superior and so skirt its western edge in September. Had some of these birds seen my house, my wife who watches them, on their way south, this, another great migration?

At the White Mallard, a little restaurant near Bayou Meto, skinny, loose-necked hounds lolligag in the sun. When I stop to ask directions, one of the hounds wanders over to me, floppy skin wattling, gravity making its eyes sad. I scratch its big ears. It dies, goes to heaven.

Bayous. Cypress trees. Hound dogs. I have reached the South, the wintering grounds. There is still room in my photo album.

Cold night air made ghosts of my breath. The forest was black, the cloud cover shielding the stars. Only against the faint grayness creeping into the clouds could I discern the naked fingers of the trees outlined overhead.

Rascal stood restlessly in the water next to me, chest-deep, shivering. Ice water lapped up to my knees, and I felt a pang of sympathy for the dog as we waited for the dawn.

In the growing light, I could make out the surface of the water, the smartweed that grew in it, and the dead and dying trees of a beaver swamp. The year had been dry, and the bottomlands were, too. No fall rain and no fall floodwaters to creep into the forest. If you wanted to hunt ducks in the timber, a local had told me, you had to find a beaver slough.

I had found this one by deceit: by spying on a pencil of light thrown by a flashlight as it bobbed through the forest, by listening to the sloshing of three hunters, and by eavesdropping on their happy conversation as they walked into the dawn. They had parked very near where I had camped in Bayou Meto, and as I stood outside the truck contemplating what the morning might bring, they disappeared into the forest. I later heard shooting.

When they returned a few hours later, wood ducks in hand, I sauntered over to chat. I think they were initially suspicious of this Yankee and his rambunctious black dog (Rascal, having listened to their shooting all morning, was absolutely wired and ready). But they warmed to me as they thawed in the sun and I probed them for advice about duck hunting in the bayou. They took me for a sunny walk in the woods, pointing out spots that normally would be good hunting in a wet year, and we sat on logs beneath the sweetgum and oak trees, talking about ducks. They were very helpful and one, very seriously, had warned me away from a particular stretch of flooded timber "where there's deep water that some hunters have disappeared into."

Now I was "kissing a tree," as they had instructed me to do: standing tight to its trunk, trying to look a part of it. In front of me, the three decoys I had thrown out swayed slightly. To the east, the sun was warning us of its coming, seeping pink into the horizon. I cradled the shotgun and listened to the echoing hoots of owls, the repeated rappings of woodpeckers, and the startling *chack!* of a mockingbird. I am not normally frightened by nature, but I wondered to myself, in the dark, whether alligators or cottonmouths were lurking nearby. In Minnesota, nothing bites but the bugs, and

ARKANSAS

they, despite what you may think at the time, are not fatal. I guessed that the unseasonably cold (for Arkansas) weather would put the reptiles to bed. I recalled a story some locals had told me about a duck hunter from Colorado who had hunted here a few years before. Taking him into the bayou, they handed him a gigantic knife in a sheath on a belt and asked him to strap it on. "What's this for?" the man had asked. "It's for the 'gators," he was told. "I'm supposed to fight a 'gator!" he exclaimed. "Naw. Just use the knife to slit those waders open once he grabs you, and then get the hell out of there." It was two days before they could convince him that they were only joking.

Far back in the bayou I heard an Arkansan warm up his duck call, producing a deep, gut-heaving grunt over the reeds. When someone from Arkansas plays a duck call, you feel the sound nearly as much as you hear it. I'm almost embarrassed to toot on my call, fearing the locals will laugh at my wimpy Minnesota duck talk.

Wings whistled somewhere. I craned my neck. Rascal's quivering picked up a few RPMs. I checked my watch. It was legal shooting time. Then *whooeek, whooeek*, and black streaks flitted through the trees, twisting like bats fetching mosquitoes. Wood ducks. I stood, mesmerized. They had come so quickly. And they had left even faster. I hadn't even moved.

Standing in this large remnant of the once vast bottomlands of the Mississippi River and its tributaries, listening to the swoops of ducks and the talking of owls, one could almost imagine that the forest went on forever, that time had stopped in this piece of primeval America. Certainly, there was enough wild country left here in Bayou Meto for a hunter to get lost in for a very long time. Bayou Meto refers not only to the brown turgid river of that name, but also to a small community on its banks and to this large, state-owned tract of public land.

Only a hundred years or so ago, the South and Southeast contained over fifty million acres of bottomland hardwood forest. In the lower Mississippi River Valley alone, what was once twenty-four million acres of this habitat was reduced to a paltry three million today. Twenty-one million acres gone.

The litany is the same here as it is in the breeding grounds: drain and convert to agriculture. The means here were different, though: channeling rivers, including the mighty Mississippi, and building levees to contain floodwaters and reservoirs to hold it back. Soybeans, cotton, and corn

replaced oaks. People moved nearer and nearer the rivers, putting false faith
in levees. Then, when nature responded with major floods, you and I
helped to rebuild their homes and levees with Federal aid. Again and again.
Perpetual and subsidized destruction.

The end result was the same as in the North: ever-shrinking habitat for
ducks and for the 270 other bird, 100 fish, and 130 mammal, reptile, and
amphibian species that call these swamps home.

Mallards and wood ducks migrate to these flooded forests each fall
(some woodies live here year round). To a lesser extent, gadwalls and green-
winged teal also winter in the swamp. Very near to where I was camped,
almost 70 percent of North America's mallards winter. Even with their
reduced numbers, this is still a breathtaking sight.

An incredibly rich ecosystem absolutely tied to the flood-and-dry
cycle, the bottomland hardwood forest functions not only as wildlife habitat but also as an important means of controlling and filtering floodwaters,
cleaning the river as silts become trapped in the forest as the water recedes.
When the waters flush the forest, they carry away great quantities of
invertebrates born in the decomposing leaf litter, thus providing nutrients
for the downstream estuaries. When the water creeps into the forest with a
fall or winter flood, the ducks gain access that they would never have risked
otherwise. Additionally, the miles of wandering waterways provide almost
unlimited sanctuary where birds can while away the winter months.

When most of us envisage a southern swamp, we see cypress trees and
to some extent tupelos draped with gray Spanish moss. Actually, these trees
make up the smallest percentage of the forest even though they are the
most water tolerant. The truly important trees are the oaks, which, unable
to withstand long periods of flooding without succumbing, grow on the
slightly higher elevations. Depending on their water tolerance, various
species of oaks grow at different elevations. Water and willow oaks stick to
the high ground; Nuttalls stay in the lowlands. Regardless of the species, the
acorns the oaks produce are the bottomland forest's true bounty, providing
nutritious food for ducks and such other creatures as deer, turkeys, and
black bears.

Very little of this habitat still exists on the much-channeled Mississippi. The remaining tracts are on national wildlife refuges, national forests,
state areas (such as Bayou Metro), and very narrow bands along streams on

private lands; they are confined now primarily to tributaries of the Father of Rivers.

I was ready when the second bunch came, swift darting ducks dressed in black in dawn's half light. There is absolutely no mistaking the wingbeat of a woodie, and sometimes you can even make out the tuft of the male's crest as it lies back in flight. Certainly, its shrill whistling call is distinctive as is its long, square tail. Wood ducks are also much smaller than mallards, the other common species of the woodlands. Almost in shifts, the wood ducks fly at dawn, and the mallards punch in a half hour later.

In every other form of duck hunting I have ever done, the ducks are always before you, over the water or decoy spread. But ducks in the tall timber fly like woodcocks, flitting through the maze of branches. Shots come from all angles, from every direction.

The first one I see is almost directly overhead. I shift my weight to my right foot, twist with my gun barrel over my left shoulder, try to remember to lead, try to pick an opening in the branches—all in four or five seconds—and then pull the trigger.

My gun sounds hollow in the swamp. Catching my balance, I watch the duck tumble, rewardingly stone dead, to the water. Having chosen to kill, I am satisfied when I make it happen cleanly.

Rascal looked up at me, almost confused. She realized, of course, that I had just shot something. But the setting was all wrong.

I pointed out the fall. "Back," I commanded.

Stained water flew as she turned toward the task. Through wetted eyeglasses I watched as she lurched, swam, humped over, and ran into stumps and submerged logs, all the time keeping to a straight line (as straight as is possible in a forest) to where the bird had splashed. And then she was coming back.

No duck is more beautiful than a male wood duck: the lemon flanks, the shimmering blue-green-black-purple head, the long swept-back crest, the chestnut breast. Gorgeous.

Interrupting my reverie, Rascal suddenly snapped left and looked skyward. I quickly put the duck in a crevice in the tree and fumbled to grasp the duck call and shotgun. The sun was now shooting clear yellow streaks of light into my eyes as it inched upward to the enveloping clouds. More wood ducks were circling.

I loved this "dismal" swamp. To prove it, I kissed the tree. This Yankee doesn't need to be told twice.

I had camped far back in Bayou Meto, nestling the camper under the massive oaks and sweetgums. The forest here is parklike, with very little undergrowth, owing, I suppose, to the periodic flooding and the fact that the stately trees block sunlight from the forest floor. Walking here is a pleasure, and after hunting in the mornings, Rascal and I would wander the higher, dry ground for miles.

In the beaver swamps where the trees have died there was a gathering of woodpeckers. Hundreds. They must winter here, too. Great concerts of rapping, staccato reverberations quivered through the still woodlands. Owls, too, found this deep forest home and at night, under the stark white moon, I would stand until I was frigid, listening as they haunted the bottomlands. Occasionally, when I answered their calls, one would work its way toward me. Once a silent owl, quiet, rounded feathers betrayed by only the whisper of a *whoosh*, glided into the glade where we were camped and perched in a branch above us. The moon threw the owl's shadow to the ground, monstrous and large on the frosted leaves, and I could see the giant head pivot and bob.

On our second night there, Rascal and I walked beneath the moon, staying on the gravel road to avoid getting lost. I saw the dog come to attention and stopped to listen. From far away I heard the music, sweet, sorrowful baying, of hounds in the forest. Rascal wanted to join them. I thought of the lazy old hounds I had seen near the White Mallard and wondered if they could possibly be the same animals now so full of voice and life. As we listened, the sound came nearer, and passed to the west of us, something out of a past I barely remember. Then they were silent, gone to the north. It was good to be in a place where man and dog still ran through the forest at night, as they had for an eternity.

Oh, the hue and cry some would voice over such a hunt with hounds! I read recently about a group of animal-rights demonstrators that had harassed a group of waterfowlers in Texas. Their goal had been to "save the ducks." Yet their organization has not contributed one cent to waterfowl-habitat work. Killing a duck is no crime; killing habitat is.

Despite being far back in the forest, we have had a few visitors. Two young men in a pick-up, flat tire flumping, pulled up to our camp as Rascal and I were having breakfast beneath the trees. One of the men quietly asked if I had a lug wrench. They had a spare and a jack but had misplaced the wrench.

I helped them change their tire, and when they were about ready to leave the same quiet fellow tried to slip a five-dollar bill in my pocket. "Take this," he said, "we appreciate you lettin' us use yo' lug ranch."

Of course, I refused the money. I told them that the next time they saw someone who needed help, to give it. That would be my payment. They protested. I protested. I won, and we were all richer.

Rascal and I were still sitting outside when an ancient pick-up with two very old black men rattled into camp a short while later. It was a scene forty years old.

We chatted. They were hunting, their battered pump shotguns, one with black tape holding its stock together, visible in the truck.

"You shoot de ducks dis mornin'?" one asked. I said that I had. A couple plump wood duck drakes.

"Man. I'd say den dat you had a good day. Dat wood duck is de bess eatin' duck in de mawsh."

I smiled. They probably thought I spoke funny too. They drove off in the old gray truck, down the wandering road. "We's jus' lookin' mo' den huntin'," one had said in answer to my question regarding their luck.

Yep, that's about the story of this grand trip I've been on. Jus' lookin' mo' den huntin'.

"Oh, would you look at that," Rick Hampton said as we stood outside his pick-up. As we looked up into a clear, cold sky, we were standing on the edge of one of the reservoirs he had built to store water to flood his rice fields.

The ducks came like meteors, falling from what must have been thousands of feet up. The specks quickly took form, their wings cupped as they dropped so rapidly that in the pit of my stomach I got that elevator feeling, just from watching. Hundreds of pintails and mallards formed a steady cascade of falling ducks that streamed into the dead, standing timber of the full reservoir.

"Man, that has got to be the greatest ride in the world," Rick said enviously, his sandy head tilted back atop his tall form.

Rick Hampton's farm is about a half hour south of Stuttgart, Arkansas (where gigantic Riceland Rice elevators stand by the railroad tracks, where every third vehicle has a Ducks Unlimited decal in the window, where camouflage clothing passes for Sunday best, and where even the radio station's call letters are KDUX), and a little south of Lodges Corner (old, white country store, paint peeling, wood floor uneven; old men in the back drinking coffee; the signs on the front door proclaiming "No Dogs Allowed," "Open Sundays during Hunting Season," and "Free Cokes Yesterday"). The attractive home and neat farm buildings sit behind a towering stand of loblolly pines. The Hamptons grow rice and soybeans. And something else.

They farm ducks, so to speak. More precisely, they grow duck habitat. I had heard of the Hamptons from a mutual acquaintance and so had stopped by. I wasn't disappointed, and I probably would have paused here even without the introduction. Any waterfowler or birder would have done so. From the road near their farm, at dusk or dawn, the passerby would see thousands upon thousands of mallards, pintails, and snow geese. Impressive.

Rick was kind enough to take me on a tour of his land. It was, like Ray Heupel's place in North Dakota, the picture of an efficient, profitable farm. But also as on Heupel's, something very obvious grabbed you: wildlife. Otters, deer, beavers, shorebirds, hawks, ducks, and geese flourished, flourished because room was made for them. Huge reservoirs, ostensibly for irrigation, were even in dry years pumped full for the birds even at considerable unreimbursed expense to Rick.

John H. Hampton, Rick's grandfather, had pioneered reservoirs; he had built the first one in about 1938, and it immediately had become a magnet for ducks.

In fact, during the tough times of the thirties, the Hamptons had practiced sound conservation measures. They filled reservoirs even in dry years, left the low rice-field levees in place to catch precipitation, and spared the bottomland forest from cultivation. The ducks, for their part, made a contribution to the Hamptons' livelihood and personal appreciation.

Here was a symbiotic relationship. You see, duck hunting has always been a part of the Hamptons' lives. In exchange for the lush habitat they provided for the birds, a small proportion of the ducks were killed, mostly by hunters who paid for the privilege. John Hampton, "the original conservationist," as Rick called him, bought his first new car for $720 with five- and ten-dollar bills collected from the hunters. This money was not gained through uncontrolled slaughter, but through careful management. Then, as now, large sections of the land, including the reservoirs, were declared off-limits to hunting, thereby providing the birds with critically needed wintering habitat. Unethical hunters were not allowed back on the land. The result of that control is apparent even today, for few places on this planet have the concentration of waterfowl that the Hampton farm does.

In addition to the benefits already described, Rick is convinced that the birds, and the winter flooding of his fields for those birds, improve his farm yields.

"Holding water on the fields saturates the soil. We get better soybean crops, and our farm is more drought-resistant," Rick said in his slow, measured southern speech. "Besides, since the ducks add natural fertilizer and eat the noxious weeds and grass we don't have to use so many chemicals and as a result have seen improved water quality. I know that because the otters have returned."

How important is private lands management to wintering waterfowl? Listen to Scott Yaich, Wetlands Coordinator at the nearby Hampton Research Center (named after Rick and his father) for the Arkansas Game and Fish Commission.

"Private lands management is vital to wintering waterfowl and to our part of the North American Plan. We are fortunate here in Arkansas that agriculture and waterfowl management aren't mutually exclusive. In a dry year like this one, the only water you'll see is either permanent or purposely flooded. Much of the latter is in farm reservoirs. People have been managing for ducks here for decades.

"We can't expect to take care of more than 20 percent of the wintering waterfowl's needs on public lands—that's a fact of life. We'll need massive involvement by the private sector. We've got a lot of interest down here by landowners who want to restore their bottomlands to hardwood forest.

They've found they can't get profitable yields in those low, wet areas anyway. By restoring them to oaks, we get habitat, and down the road, they'll get a financial return from some timber production.

"We also need to convince the farmers to not plow their rice stubble and levees under so they'll hold water, like what the Hamptons do. A guy can grow a full rice crop, doing nothing differently than he normally does, and, by reflooding the fields in the winter, provide super waterfowl habitat. But that'll be the bottleneck, too, because managing water is very expensive. We know there are benefits to both the farmers and ducks. But educating everyone to that, and finding the money for all of this, are the real issues."

Rick and I walked along the reservoir levee in the late-afternoon light. Ducks, almost oblivious to our presence, still dropped from the heights.

"Can you walk a pipe?" Rick asked, pointing at an irrigation pipeline over a ditch. He deftly pranced across. I followed, making it across even with the slippery Arkansas mud clinging to the soles of my boots. We stood quietly watching the ducks.

"It costs us a lot of money to flood the fields, but we do it for the ducks. My grandfather always said that we have paradise right here at home. He was right."

From a dizzying height the ducks continued to drop, bellies full, no doubt, of rice gleaned from nearby fields.

Rick, still gazing upward, softly said, "I believe they're having fun. I believe I would."

And I thought, yup, when I die, send me to Stuttgart, Arkansas.

It was late afternoon. Rick had dropped Rascal and me off about a half mile from his home. Rick had graciously offered to let me hunt from his pit. To have come all the way to the flooded fields of Arkansas and not have spent an hour over decoys would have been something I'd regret all my life. I quickly accepted.

Rascal and I slogged across the slippery flats through shin-deep water. A concrete pit with a thatched hatch sat low in one of the levees. Decoys were floating all around; some sat on the levees themselves. I persuaded Rascal to lie down on the muddy ground outside the pit and then eased myself inside.

When the sun slanted low and the air began to cool, the ducks came in black flocks of hundreds and hundreds, silhouetted against the smoky gold sunset. Millions of mallards winter here, and I was seeing a large slice of that population. Pintails came, too, their long necks and pointed tails distinctive.

You might think it would be easy to kill ducks here, but on this day the big flocks so outnumbered the decoy spread that they were little inclined to drop in. Still, despite my Minnesota duck calling, a few birds gave us a close look, and when they did I peered through the thatching and watched the swiveling heads, heard a hen or two, and tried to start up a conversation. Rascal lay motionless except for that big, black head that craned to watch the birds.

Being virtually underground, almost at water level, provides an interesting perspective from which to watch waterfowl. Sometimes the birds were on top of us before I ever saw them. They came from behind, their only warning the *whew-whew-whew* of wings. Hundreds went by before I gave a thought to shooting.

To my right outside the pit I saw Rascal tense, claws gripping mud, like a cat, and I knew there must be birds in range. Throwing the hatch open, I stood up, saw two hundred mallards floating into the decoys in slow motion, red legs spraddled. They were soon aware of me and of their mistake. I had hoped for this chance, had saved two of my three-bird daily limit in case Rick invited me to hunt his fields. I threw the old Browning up, felt the stock against my shoulder, picked a rusty-chested greenhead, and aimed beneath his descending form.

The roar of the gun caused a thunder of flapping, flashing wings as mallards wildly changed directions, nearly colliding in their escape. I saw another greenhead, climbing nose to the sky. I pointed the barrel above him, fired, saw him quiver, fired again, and watched him fall to the brown water. I set the gun down.

Rascal exploded with my command, made short work of the easy retrieves, and splashed back to me with the huge drakes, water flying from her prancing feet. We sat on the edge of the pit, done with hunting, no longer worried about concealment. I stroked the wet dog, smelling that good odor of wet retriever, and watched the setting sun. The air grew suddenly chill, and the great flocks of ducks headed to the Hamptons' reservoirs for the night.

I picked up the ducks and my gear and walked toward Rick's waiting truck, using its headlights as my guide. Overhead, the whirring of wings still could be heard.

"Did you enjoy that?" Rick asked as we sat in the warm truck.

"Your grandfather was right," I said after thanking him. "This is paradise."

LOUISIANA

The birds, Rascal, and I are on the wintering grounds. Southerners must surely be cursing me because I had brought winter with me. When I left Bayou Meto, the swamps were frozen, and snow, a rarity there, lay two inches thick. The roads through beautiful piney Mississippi were treacherous with ice. Cars and trucks were carcasses in the ditches.

We inched along the slippery roads, in and out of small towns, pecans for sale everywhere, po' boy sandwiches (submarines, or hoagies, to some of us) available at every stop, catfish dinners a delight.

While many a dabbling duck spends the winter in the remaining bottomland swamps, many others, as well as a great number of the diving ducks, push on to the coastal marshes that span from East Texas across Louisiana and into Mississippi. Anywhere from fifty to seventy-five miles deep, this incredible wetland encompasses some two million acres, 40 percent of America's coastal marshes, and is the winter home to more than 50 percent of the Mississippi Flyway's ducks and great numbers of its snow geese. Some do not stop here but instead overfly the broad Gulf of Mexico to South America or head inland to the wetlands of Mexico. Rascal and I would call our journey to an end when we could taste the salt in the air.

By mid-December, we have come a long, weary, exalting way. We had crossed the Mississippi River six times and had seen prairies, forests, bottomlands, and rice fields.

Once in Louisiana the very sound of the world changed, more foreign to a northerner than Canada had been. Names like Tangipahoa, Ticfaw, and Bogue Chitto rolled by as Rascal and I pushed on, north of Lake Pontchartrain to Slidell. Her head still on my lap, Rascal has patiently accompanied me for eight thousand wandering miles.

Slidell sits just across Lake Pontchartrain from New Orleans (NAWlenz, as the locals say). Never have I seen a place where *zoning* must be a dirty word. Houses sit next to shopping malls, which sit next to industrial complexes, which sit next to condominiums. When I mentioned this phenomenon to a native, he simply said, "Zonin' is jus' too much guvmint."

We found a cheap motel and checked in, tired. I took Rascal for a walk nearby and found a patch of woods. The air was warm and moist; the small gnats droned in our ears. I learned quickly that the soil is moist, too; although it appeared dry and grassy, it quickly sucked at my shoes. I found out that in places this area is below sea level.

Hungry, Rascal and I headed into New Orleans and found our way to the French Quarter. I parked the truck, left the dog, and wandered around. A fat black man in a Santa suit stood on a street corner, playing incredible jazz versions of Christmas tunes on a saxophone. I bounced around the wonderful shops and restaurants, bought some gifts for Mary Jo, gorged myself on Creole chicken, seafood, and beer.

The dark, narrow streets were alive with people. Old brick buildings huddled right up to the streets, their wrought iron verandas terracing above. Jazz and wonderful food odors wafted out every open door and window. To this backward boy from Minnesota, the French Quarter seemed like another continent.

In the dark, with loaded shopping bags and a full stomach, I returned to listen to the fat black Santa of Decatur Street one more time and then, weariness weighing down my eyelids, drove back to the motel, windows open to keep me awake, the smell of salt in the air.

In the motel, I took my first shower in days while Rascal ate. Then I crawled into bed. I had turned out all lights but the one next to the bed, and in the dark I noticed something crawling along the floor. Rascal pounced on it. A cockroach. She lifted her paws, and it scooted under the desk. Another one was on a nearby wall. Yet another was making tracks toward Rascal's dish. Great. I had booked a room at the Roach Motel.

I turned out the light and called Rascal up onto the bed, hoping the roaches didn't follow. I would try to sleep with my mouth shut.

Crisp salt air stung my nostrils. Standing in a marsh on the outskirts of New Orleans, we listened to the morning come to life. Despite the cool temperature, there was a lushness here I had never experienced. At home, snow lay on the ground, had for a month. But from where we stood I could look over acres of waving grass, the tallest phragmites I'd ever seen, and see oaks and willows still with green leaves. A low flight of pelicans cruised by on the blushing horizon.

Dave Hall stood next to me, his arm sweeping over the marsh as he talked. This sixteen-hundred-acre area, he explained, was being considered for an urban wildlife refuge. In midsentence he cut his explanation short, abbreviated by the punctuation of shotgun blasts.

U.S. Fish and Wildlife Service Special Agent Hall turned his ear to the wind. His Deep South relaxed demeanor vanished; his eyes lit up. As I watched, I could see he was counting the shots, timing the spacing. When the shooting ended he spoke.

"Oh, those boys better cut it out. They're doing bad. Killing way too many ducks. Boy, I'd sure like to know how they got out there. I'll have to come back here with my pirogue."

Though someone was shooting too many ducks, I couldn't help but feel thrilled. I had just witnessed a first-rate predator at work, a predator who preys on poachers. And I for one was damn glad he was on the side of the law. How he could ever judge that "those boys" were doing bad just by listening, I couldn't guess. But I didn't doubt his judgment for a moment.

We returned to Dave's Suburban (the vehicle had been confiscated from politicians who had used it for hauling illegal quantities of crappie to Chicago) and turned back to the highway. A mile down the levee, Dave spotted two hunters pulling pirogues (crafts similar to dug out canoes) out of the marsh.

Hall climbed out of the unmarked truck and announced himself to the hunters. He inquired about their success.

"Eet was great," said a swarthy Cajun. "Der were duck flying everywhere. Dis bunch juz come to de decoy as I sit still in my pirogue. An I was in de open." He held up his birds. He had three, his legal limit. Hall was smiling. These were not the boys we had heard "doing bad." They were the fruits of his efforts. Boys doing good: hunting legally, and loving it.

"Take their picture, Mike." Dave instructed. "I want you to show people that Louisiana hunters aren't all outlaws."

I took the picture, and we traveled on toward Bayou LaFourche, driving along swampy Louisiana marshes and past heaps of litter and debris. Egrets and herons stood among garbage-filled waterways. If littering isn't the state pastime, it is at least a serious hobby. A beautiful place like Louisiana deserves much better.

As we drove, I got a feel for Dave Hall. He had been with the Service for twenty-nine years, serving in almost every part of the nation. He was trained as a biologist and worked first in refuges. He also worked waterfowl surveys in Canada for many years. As he saw what was happening to North America's wildlife, he became convinced that he could do more good in law enforcement than in research. Many studies, he believes, are repetitive and unnecessary. When it was announced recently that there was to be a study of canvasback diets in the wintering grounds of south Louisiana,

Poaching

The true scope of the waterfowl-poaching problem is unknown, but in recent years the tolerance for such illegal acts has declined dramatically, motivated in part by concern for the dwindling duck population.

Poaching goes on wherever ducks concentrate. Typical offenses down the flyway during the migration include taking too many birds, killing the wrong species or sex, and shooting legal limits more than once a day. Poachers along the migration route are limited by opportunity, since the ducks are present in significant numbers for a relatively short period of time.

The worst cases of poaching occur in the wintering areas. Poachers in Chesapeake Bay and other east-coast marshes place grain in the water or field to attract waterfowl. Baiting, as this practice is known, is illegal.

Southern wintering grounds, by their remote nature and large concentrations of waterfowl, have historically experienced the worst large-scale poaching. Estimates for Louisiana poaching, made by the U.S. Fish and Wildlife Service, indicate that the illegal kill of ducks may have been as high as four times the legal harvest. Much of this abuse was carried on in private "hunting" reserves, often run by wealthy corporations. Baiting is a common practice on these reserves.

Greater efforts in enforcement, increasingly severe penalties, and widespread publicity and education have served to reduce the effects of poaching on waterfowl populations.

Dave told the researcher to take out a pen and paper. "I told them right then what they'd find," he said angrily at the thought of the U.S. government's killing rare canvasback ducks for what he feels is needless research.

He is also a thoughtful man. On the plight of wetlands and waterfowl: "It's going to boil down to not just protecting wetlands for ducks and duck hunters, but also for the benefit of all of society. We need places to get back to our roots. There is nothing so therapeutic as being out of doors."

On why he does what he does: "If I never shot another duck or caught another fish—gosh, what I've already seen out in the marsh. I need to put something back."

About development and religion: "I hate the term 'developing nation' and the way we send missionaries to them. We hear so much about how Africa is destroying its wildlife. People should look around. We're doing worse right here in America. We ought to be ashamed of ourselves. Look how we've destroyed the cultures of the Indians and Eskimos. The religion of the American Indian made more sense than any other religion. Now those people have nothing. Who are we to tell them their ways are wrong?"

The green bayou swept up to the highway. Dave pulled quickly to the side, turned the truck around, and pulled into a driveway. What had caught his attention I didn't know until he slowed to a stop. I saw two pirogues pulled onto the bank. An old man walked up to Dave's open window and they started chatting. The man was cautious, but Dave's easy way wore him down.

"Dey was a bunch of de guys back dere dis mornin'," he said in his heavy accent and with a wave toward the marsh. "Dey shore do a lot of shootin'. I bet dey shoot two box worth. I axe dem if dey get many duck. Dey say dey was jus' practice shootin'," he laughs.

We laugh too. The man sells vegetables from a stand on the highway and tells Dave and me to stop back and pick some up with his compliments on our way home.

Away from the old man, the laughing ceases. "They weren't practice shooting. They were screwing up, I'll guarantee you that. I'll be back," Dave said seriously, the predator surfacing again.

I was confused about these Cajuns. They seemed genuinely friendly, warm, and carefree. How is it, then, that they were capable of such huge duck kills, such great violations of the laws? Dave had once estimated that the illegal duck kill in Louisiana alone might be four times the legal harvest.

"These people are proud and honest. Their heritage proves this. But they have been isolated by language and the land," Hall said.

The Cajun people are descendents of the French who, beginning in 1604, settled in what is now Nova Scotia but was at the time known as Acadia. When Acadia became a territory of the British empire, the Acadians were ruthlessly harassed by the British colonists.

Beginning in 1755, the British forced the Acadians from their homes. The Acadians migrated to several places, but many wound up in the vast marshes, prairies, and bayous of Louisiana. Infinitely resourceful and able to endure great hardship, they clung to their culture and language in this strange but bountiful land. They were primarily fisher folk, but also used many of the land's other resources. Like the American Indians, they found that all they needed lay near at hand in the form of plants, animals, waterfowl, and fishes. The term Cajun now applies not only to those of Acadian ancestry, but also to anyone who has married into those families.

"Their skills in hunting ducks are unsurpassed," Dave explained. "And in their culture they use everything and share everything. Ducks are never wasted."

In other words, they had the ability to kill many ducks. They also had the opportunity due to the large wintering population of birds. And because the supply seemed endless and there were so many poor neighbors in the bayou that would eat as many as you could bring back, a skilled hunter was a hero, not a poacher—no matter what the laws said.

But times changed. In the past couple of decades, Cajuns have been lured away from working in the marsh to toiling in the oil fields. Outsiders came in. Wealthy "sportsmen" leased huge areas (twenty-five thousand to fifty thousand acres) for duck hunting. The canals dug in the coastal marshes for oil rigs let in salt water, killing the three-square grass, live oaks, and freshwater marsh plants, seriously limiting wintering areas and encouraging widespread erosion of these vital marshes.

The duck killing went on in huge numbers, but not just by the Cajuns who had the marginal excuse of being able to use the ducks. The killing went on at large private clubs when duck numbers were spiraling downward and it went on at a time when wintering habitat was vanishing. Baiting with grain became more and more common, often during hunts organized by big corporations to "treat" their clients. The killing went on in all its ruthlessness. And it was protected by a moral code that had started with the simple Cajun life-style of utilizing and sharing the resource, a code that had not evolved fast enough to keep up with the changes.

Dave Hall knew that something drastic had to be done. Diligently, he moved the agencies responsible for protecting ducks toward developing an effective deterrent to these crimes. At times he was chastised by his own agency for his zealousness and made enemies in national conservation organizations, which had members of high rank participating in the kills. But he found support among the true sportsmen of Louisiana and the rest of the nation and within the field ranks of the USFWS and state conservation officers. It took time, effort, and most critically, the changing of attitudes. Changing the attitudes of adults was something everyone told

Hall he couldn't do. They told him he'd have to work on the kids, wait a generation. Hall, fortunately, didn't believe them.

"You can't tell a culture they are wrong by laws alone. You have to give them options," he said. "You have to convince them that you're not arresting people to make their lives miserable but that you're doing it for a cause, a cause that is right. Only then can you be effective as a game law-enforcement agent."

When a corporation was convicted of allowing overkill at its duck camp, part of its penalty was to provide filmmaking equipment to Dave. Dave's plan was to use videotape to document the problem and to educate the public, the ethical hunter, and even the violators about the seriousness of the crimes. Into the swamps he went, taping busts and interviewing outlaws. The change this tool had made was evident during my visit. Attitudes had been modified. Gross overbagging was way down, and so was baiting. Ex-violators became Dave's best pitchmen. Finally, compliance with the laws increased, and people began to see the wealth of waterfowl and wetlands with a new perspective.

After years of making busts, Dave knew that the old system didn't work. Writing tickets, he argues, isn't the purpose of law enforcement; increasing compliance is. By creating a deterrent through strong, fair enforcement coupled with creative and sometimes severe court sentencing, and developing a strong educational effort, he had proven that this new direction works. He became a man with a mission.

"I could have retired, but I got involved in this program," he said. "I've never been more enthused about educating people about wildlife laws. The duck hunters I've seen in the past two years have been obeying the laws better and enjoying the experience more than in all my other years as an agent."

While touring the bayous with Dave, I spoke to many Cajuns, some whose past included an arrest by Agent Hall. Two things were evident. First, attitudes had changed, sometimes from a newfound appreciation for ducks and sometimes from the fear of being caught and punished. Second, they respected Dave Hall. They knew that he was a man who was honest and would track them down no matter where in the bayou they hid. When Agent Hall busted you, you had no excuses. You'd been "screwing up," and you knew it.

"The Cajun people know we are right, and they respect that. I knew we were making progress when these people started inviting us to their Mardi Gras," Hall said.

As if to prove the effectiveness of this new program, one man confided this: "This year I even turned in my own brother-in-law. He took his son and my son hunting and shot a limit in the morning and another in the evening. I finally had it. It has to end."

Hall and I stopped for coffee (they call it coffee in Louisiana but I suspect it's oil-rig sludge) and doughnuts. As we stood at the counter, chatting and ordering, Dave elbowed me and snapped "hush." I listened. In a booth nearby three men were talking. One said, "My boy, he was pinched de oder day by de warden. Dey is everywhere dese day an dey don' even wear de uniform or have marked cars. Use to be you could call someone, have de thing taken care of, but no more."

As we drove away, Dave smiled at me, pleased at what we had just heard. "It's a thrill for me to know I had a part in taming the 'Wild West.' That's what this has been all about."

The analogy was appropriate. The sheriff made a cowtown safe for good people. Dave Hall, his program, and those who helped him had made the marshes a little safer for the ducks. Too many times, though, in those old movies, the good guy rode away before being thanked. I didn't want that to happen this time.

Thanks, Dave. Thanks from all of us who love "de duck."

In the half-light of dawn, the noisy mudboat came to a halt. Burly Jay Duet, his close-cropped black beard hugging his round, swarthy face, slid the pirogue I was to use into the water, over the mudboat's transom. He tossed out some decoys and put a push-pole and paddle in the pirogue.

Looking at Rascal and me, he said, "De pirogue is a tippy boat. De dog, she ride in it?"

I said she would. In fact, she was only too happy to get out of the mudboat. (The day before, frightened by the boat's loud Chevy engine, Rascal had piled over the gunwale into the canal. Jay had smiled dryly and said, "She's a good duck dog. You can't keep her out of de water.")

I patted the pirogue and told Rascal to kennel up. As she has done a thousand times into my canoe back home, she deftly leaped into the pirogue and lay down on the center line. I stepped in, grabbed my gun from the mudboat, and poled off to the duck blind, the black ooze of the marsh bottom sucking at the push-pole. Progress was painfully slow, but we finally pulled the pirogue into the blind. (Cajun blinds are fascinating and nearly invisible. In this one you simply pulled yourself, boat and all, through a narrow opening and then stuck your head through the woven grass opening that arched over the framework.)

The cold, strong wind that had blown from the north all night had carried much of the marsh's water out to the Gulf. Mud flats appeared everywhere.

Rascal and I sat and watched for the dawn. To the east, huge clouds of ducks that were roused by the passage of Jay's boat swirled above the rusty horizon. A flock of graceful, curve-billed ibis, white in the gray light, flew over us on powerful, quiet wings. Rascal started as sandpipers, flitting like a dark mass of blackbirds, whipped past our ears to set down on the exposed mud. White pelicans came in vee formation. A nutria wallowed out of the water to sit munching vegetation across the narrow strip of water where our decoys bobbed.

The coastal marshes looked somber but very much alive. It was hard to believe that they were disappearing, that they may in fact disappear almost completely in my lifetime. The water here was brackish. Jesse Duet, the old Cajun gentleman at whose camp we were staying, had told me that in his youth the water here had been so clear and clean that you could drink it, that water lilies bloomed, that frogs and alligators and water moccasins and bass made it their home, that his father could trap as many as five hundred muskrats a day, and that "you could run across dat marsh."

One day twenty years earlier, Dave Hall had used a helicopter to descend on Jesse, who had been a notorious duck killer. After checking Jesse's kill, Dave told him that within his lifetime he'd see this marsh disappear, that it would all become salt water.

And Jesse had replied, "Mr. Hall, you might know de duck, but you sure don' know anything about de marsh. It'll be here long after I'm gone."

As he told me this story last night, Jesse added sadly, "You know what, everything he said came true. De marsh is dying."

The marsh began to die when the Army Corps of Engineers channelized the last miles of the Mississippi River. The coastal marshes had been formed when the ever-changing river spewed vast loads of silt across the delta and changed its exit repeatedly over time. The fresh water and yearly supply of silt and the periodic flooding and flushing created the coastal marshes and kept them alive. Without the Mississippi the marshes slowly began to die, and the rich silt flowed wastefully into the Gulf of Mexico.

The final straw came with the reckless granting of permits to the oil companies who wanted to drill in the marshes. Although the construction of shell roads would have been less destructive, huge waterways were built to facilitate the movement of heavy equipment and oil rigs. Lured by profits and jobs, the big companies and the often corrupt Louisiana government mercilessly began to dismember the wetlands. Though some might consider oil exploration within such valuable wetlands cause enough for despair, the real damage was from the canals. Salt water, which is heavier than fresh water, began to intrude upon the sea-level marshes, pushing deeper and deeper into the wetlands. By doing so, it killed all the salt-water-intolerant plants and drove out the birds, mammals, reptiles, and fish that depended upon those plants. Once the plants died, the roots that held the marsh together vanished, too. With every new storm on the Gulf, huge chunks of marsh vanished overnight. Now, up to fifty square miles disappear each year. Half of the Mississippi Delta, which has been accumulating since the year 1400, has been lost in the past twenty-five years.

As I watched the huge conglomeration of seabirds and shorebirds wheeling on the wind, the clouds of ducks rowing on the cold breeze, I found it incomprehensible that as a nation we would allow such an important wetland to vanish merely for expedience and profit. Then I recalled the potholes of the north and realized that the games don't change, just the players do.

Rascal and I scanned the slate sky. Ever hopeful, I watched as a flock of gadwalls worked their way toward me.

We had come to the end of our trip. We had seen the coastal marshes.

Jesse Duet is a piece of work. Short, powerfully built, still robust in his seventies, he has lived his life in the bayou. His camp, located on a high strip of land surrounded by his two square miles of marsh, is his haven, complete with boats, pirogues, stray cats, and two burly Labradors.

Jesse had killed a lot of ducks in his day, maybe more than anyone else alive. If you think of him as a bloodthirsty killer though, you are very wrong.

Years earlier, Jesse and his family killed many ducks, poule d'eau (coots), and gros-bec (night herons) to eat.

"My mother would send me out with two shells and I would shoot maybe fifty, sixty duck and poule d'eau with dem, you know, by killing dem on de water. But dat was our food. I'd gut dem and hang dem in de shade, and we'd eat dem for a week."

But that ethic did not change along with the world that was rapidly evolving. For Jesse, getting arrested helped to change his ways. Later, Jesse and Dave Hall became best friends. For Dave Hall was different. In the old days, state wardens simply looked the other way if Jesse would give them half of his kill.

"I'd shoot fifty duck, knowing de warden, he would be waitin' for me at camp. I'd give him twenty-five, and he'd leave me alone."

Dave Hall's passion for ducks and their protection allowed him to convince Jesse that the old ways were now wrong. And Jesse, keen and bright, had begun to admit to himself that the marsh was changing, that duck numbers were declining. Getting a man like Jesse Duet on your side was a boon to Hall. Respected among the other Cajuns, Jesse could help to spread the message. Jesse loves ducks, and Dave's arguments deeply affected him.

We stood on the porch of his camp, looking out over perhaps four hundred acres of open water in the marsh. Ducks of every kind traded on the wind.

"Der mus' be twenty-five thousan' duck dere," Jesse said. "An I don' let nobody shoot dem duck. That's der sanctuary. Dey know if dey can get into dis hole, dey got it made," he said proudly, his eyes shining behind glasses, his gray hair blowing in the cold, December wind. "But I got guys on my ass. You bet I do. Dey want to shoot dem duck, and I won't let dem."

Like Ray Heupel and Rick Hampton, Jesse Duet was a landowner determined to make a difference. A life of trapping, hunting, and fishing had stirred in him a great love for the marsh. The marsh had been good to him, and he had, at times, abused it. But a smart person knows when he has made a mistake, and a brave one can admit to it. Jesse is both.

"You see de duck," Jesse said, his thick arm pointing over the marsh. "I'd like my grandchildren to see de same thing. I still hunt de duck, but I don' shoot many now."

At dark, just before we turned to go into the warm cabin, Jesse stopped to look wistfully at the waves of ducks one more time.

"I don' own de duck, but I sure will try to protect dem."

Rascal and I sit in yet another of Jesse's wonderful invisible duck blinds. It is dark, and cold enough to snow. What the hell have I done, brought winter with me? My new Cajun friends will never invite me back.

The Cajuns are wonderful people. I love their food. We ate roast teal and goose; blackened redfish that Jay cooked outside in an enormous skillet the size of a trash-can lid, so smoky you don't dare cook indoors; spicy boudin sausage made of pork, rice, onions, and seasoning stuffed into intestines; red beans and rice—the perfect food; spicy shrimp with rice and well-seasoned eggs that Jesse cooks in the predawn, shuffling around in slippers, while I watch, sipping on a cup of thick, black Cajun coffee guaranteed to wake up a corpse.

I love the way their rich language rhythmically slips off the tongue. They have grand names for ducks: mallard, *canard francais*; ringneck, *t' canard noir*; wigeon, *zan zan*; teal, *t' congo*.

And I love the way that Jesse's camp—low, green, and framed by the tall phragmites that glow yellow in the setting sun—sits on the edge of the canal where boats are ready, duck dogs race on the lawn, herons and pelicans flap by, and long rows of graceful ibis stream against the brilliant sunset. I have come and met what Dave Hall calls "the finest people in America." I have seen the giant oaks of the South, trees that are four hundred years old and so big around that four people can't hold hands to encircle them. I have seen the old black women in straw hats walk down to the canals, cane poles in one hand, bucket in the other. I have seen ducks, too.

We've come a long way: across most of a continent, past prairies, down rivers, and through heat and snow. The teal came first, even before I left home, seeking the coastal marshes as early as August. But the mallards, pintails, gadwalls, and all the rest of our companions arrived just before we did, in November; some are coming still.

We'll be leaving soon. But the ducks will stay all winter, to depart in February or March on favorable winds. Many of them will already be paired when they seek the potholes of the north. I envy them their luxury of a winter in this beautiful place. And I will miss seeing them during the long winter months.

Shivering, Jesse dropped us off in this, one of his best blinds, determined that I get in some of the duck shooting for which Louisiana is so famous.

We watched the dawn for one last time. With it came the battalions of shorebirds and the garrisons of seabirds. And then the ducks came. They flew low, for the sky was scraping the reed tops. The morning was so dark that sunrise meant almost nothing, the wind would stir the heart of a duck hunter long dead.

Outside the tiny blind Rascal sat enthralled, a black statue in the gloom. *Zan zan* raced on the wind, saw the bobbing decoys, and swung around. I watched as they set their wings, and when a bright male passed near, I dumped him into the black water. A second one, confused, sailed back over the blind, and he too met his end. I whispered "back" to Rascal as I pointed out the first duck, and she hit the water with enthusiasm and caught up with the drifting bird as the wind blew it far down the marsh. The second retrieve came easier.

When the gadwalls came, I was waiting. One more bird to make my limit, one last bird to take home. The unwary and unwise die first in all species, as did the brazen gadwall that streaked into the decoys. When I fired, it tipped end over end and landed upright, still alive. Rascal sat tight, waiting for the command. For the last time, I leaned over a duck blind to give her a line to the retrieve with the edge of my hand.

I heard a rattling in my pocket and paused, telling the dog to stay. I reached in and fumbled for the canister. It was Gypsy, my old, dear friend. She, too, had come to the end of the flyway with me. She would have loved it here, I thought.

Rascal whimpered. The duck was disappearing across the marsh. My dumb fault. The retrieve would be difficult now. If she needed help I wouldn't be able to do a thing, for Jesse had dropped me off without a pirogue.

Of course. Gypsy could help. One last retrieve for Gypsy. I pried open the lid, sprinkled the white ashes and grit of my absent friend down the wet, quivering spine of my new companion.

"Gypsy, Rascal. Back."

I sent them both on the retrieve and sat down in the blind, tears in my eyes. The north wind blew hard, ducks in its grasp streaming past me. Rascal caught up to the gadwall, grabbed it as it tried to dive, and turned back, without Gypsy.

I finally said goodbye to Gypsy. We had reached the end of our trip.

As if he had been watching me, as soon as the third bird was retrieved Jesse appeared across the marsh, motoring into the wind.

He picked me up and smiled at my success. We headed across the great coastal marsh to the warmth of the camp. No matter where I looked, birds—ducks, geese, sandpipers, terns, ibis—were in the air.

Jesse motored into the boathouse. I climbed out, hung my ducks in the rafters, and walked to the canal's bank to look out upon the day. The north wind stung my face. Rascal sat by my side.

It was over.

EPILOGUE

Rascal and I—and the ducks and the geese—have traveled south across a varied and beautiful landscape on the wings of a north wind. We have seen where the ducks come from and where they go.

What we had at the advent of civilizing this continent we will never have again. What we had even a century ago we will never see again. But what we have now, even in its diminished state, is still a splendor to behold, a treasure that needs to be cherished.

The values that were used to open this continent have now outlived their usefulness. Subduing land instead of recognizing that we are a part of it has been the norm. That attitude should now be considered criminal.

We have a tendency to relegate to the government important tasks regarding our environment. In reality, since each one of us is the problem, we are all responsible. Until we demand that the land and its diverse communities be treated with care, the loss of wetlands and other important habitats will continue. A land ethic must become a part of our national mentality. The public policies that have allowed the destruction need to be changed. Indeed, since so much of what has been lost has come about with public approval and funds, there is hope that new policies enacted by an enlightened people can reverse the trend and restore some of the bounty of the past.

We are guilty of measuring life merely by goods and profits. We have traded natural wealth for material wealth. And with each day, there are more of us. Our population grows unchecked and with it our needs, both real and imagined.

What of the waterfowl and other creatures that enrich our lives and stir our souls? Have we lost our need for such things? If we have, what will be our inspiration? New cars? Rows of buildings?

Restoring ducks may be accomplished by managing them as a crop: crowding them onto reserves and intensively controlled breeding areas, as on national wildlife refuges and in Ducks Unlimited projects. These procedures are sometimes necessary as stopgap measures. But to look to such projects as the future is to point out our wrongmindedness in believing that ducks, and life in general, can be perpetuated on ecological islands. To seriously pursue such a course means, in essence, that we have forfeited any chance to develop a true land ethic.

I wish I were optimistic about the prospects. The key to saving most wildlife and to improving the health of all ecosystems is in the hands of the individual. And while I have met great and generous people along the way, people who are willing to share their land with nature or who are struggling to educate the public, the fact remains that the vast majority of people I passed are neither concerned nor likely to become so.

Nearly every biologist I met volunteered the thought that we are in the midst of the final battle. This is our last chance to ensure that large populations of wild, free-ranging waterfowl will exist.

Will we change the policies of destruction? Will we educate ourselves about a land ethic? Will we divest ourselves of the arrogant pride that sets us first, and therefore apart, from the rest of nature? Each one of us must answer those questions. If most of us answer yes, then wildlife has a future.

Someday, perhaps fifty years from now, someone may take this volume down from a library shelf, blow the dust from its edges, and read it. And perhaps when he is finished he will smile, thankful that we changed things in time, that we saved what was left of our wetlands and waterfowl.

I hope so. I really do.

About the Author

Michael Furtman is a writer and photographer who often takes as his subject matter the Minnesota wilderness. He is an active member of the Izaak Walton League and frequently works with the U.S. Forest Service. He has written two books, *A Boundary Waters Fishing Guide* (1984) and *A Season For Wilderness* (1989), as well as articles for *Field and Stream, Sports Afield, Canoe, Wildfowl, Fly-Fisherman*, and many other national and regional publications. A life-long resident of Duluth, Furtman lives with his wife, Mary Jo, and Labrador, Rascal.

Other Stackpole books for waterfowlers

Aldo Leopold's Wilderness
Selected Early Writings by the Author of
A Sand County Almanac
Edited with interpretive comments by David E. Brown and
Neil B. Carmony
Aldo Leopold, father of ecology and proponent of a wilderness ethic, explores the concepts that inspired the environmental movement.
Hardcover, $18.95, Canada $25.50

Fireside Waterfowler
Fundamentals of Duck and Goose Ecology
Edited by David E. Wesley and William G. Leitch
This fact-filled book from Ducks Unlimited will increase your knowledge and enjoyment of the waterfowl resource we all cherish.
Hardcover, $29.95, Canada $39.95

Ducks, Geese and Swans of North America
by Frank C. Bellrose, Jr.
The award-winning standard authority on all North American waterfowl species. Over 200,000 copies in print.
Hardcover, $39.95, Canada $49.95

Making Decoys
The Century-Old Way
by Grayson Chesser and Curtis J. Badger
Detailed, step-by-step instructions for carving and painting simple yet functional working decoys.
Hardcover, $24.95, Canada $33.50

Brown Feathers
Waterfowling Tales and Upland Dreams
by Steven J. Mulak
Wit and wisdom, pleasure and poignancy: 27 stories of hunters and dogs and birds afield.
Hardcover, $16.95, Canada $22.95

American Duck Shooting
by George Bird Grinnell
First published in 1901, this classic examines more than fifty species of waterfowl and the methods used to hunt and conserve them. Third book in the *Classics of American Sport* series.
Paperback, $17.95, Canada $24.50

Sporting Clays
Expert Techniques for Every Kind of Clays Course
by Michael Pearce
Thorough and tested instructions on how to shoot all types of targets with finesse.
Hardcover, $16.95, Canada $22.95